THE OFFICIAL

DOWNTON ABBEY

COCKTAIL BOOK

FOREWORD BY JULIAN FELLOWES

weldon**owen**

TABLE *of* CONTENTS

FOREWORD

Cocktails were slow to make an appearance on *Downton Abbey* but make no mistake: the Crawleys love to drink. In season 1, Robert Crawley regularly enjoys Scotch, dinners begin and end with sherry and port, parties include alcoholic punches, and plenty of wine and Champagne is poured—but none of the Crawleys or their servants sips a cocktail. The fact is, drinking before dinner did not begin until the end of the First World War and so the steady creep of cocktails into *Downton Abbey* only starts in seasons 2 and 3, when Robert asks his mother, Violet, "Can I tempt you to one of these new cocktails?" At this point, fashionable members of London society were beginning their evenings with a cocktail, a custom Lady Rose implores Robert to adopt. She is an early enthusiast, and Lady Edith gladly raises a glass once she begins making regular trips to London. Happily for Lady Rose—and the rest of the family—over the course of the show's remaining seasons, cocktails make more than a cameo appearance; they are, in fact, a mainstay of the household's dining and entertaining protocol. Edith, in particular, as a young career woman and urbanite, drinks them a great deal, in her flat, in restaurants, and at Downton itself, where cocktails are well established by the final episode. It takes newcomer Henry Talbot, however, to introduce the cocktail shaker.

This lively compendium is a celebration of the best cocktails of the *Downton Abbey* era and beyond. It is replete with recipes, cocktail trivia, historical notes, and excerpts from the show, and I hope you will find there is much here to savour.

JULIAN FELLOWES
LONDON, MAY 2019

"THERE'S NEVER A DULL MOMENT IN THIS HOUSE"

Drinking is very important at Downton. At least three types of wine are served at every upstairs dinner, plus port for the gentlemen after it. There's alcoholic punch at parties, plenty of Champagne, and, as the years go by, the gradual adoption of the cocktail. Mixed drinks are first mentioned in season 2, and it takes until the last season for one of the family—in this case Henry Talbot—to wield a cocktail shaker, but they lurk in the background of many a party. Edith, in particular, who, after Gregson leaves her his flat, lives a more modern life than her sisters as a bachelorette, is a serial quaffer of Champagne, G&Ts, and cocktails at various venues across London. Rose, representing a slightly younger and cooler dynamic than most of the rest of the family, is also no stranger to cocktails, which are regarded as decidedly "fast" by most others.

Cocktails were essentially an American import, and it's no surprise that the Dowager Countess wages a private war against them. When the show opens, dinners are very Victorian in style, and the predinner cocktail is unknown. The half hour before dinner was termed by one writer of the time as the hostess's "greatest ordeal," as she waited, no drink in hand, to see if the dinner was going to be a success or not. By the last season, the Dowager Countess has been beaten, and cocktails of many different hues are a mainstay.

Wine, of which Violet definitely approves, was usually French or German on country house tables. Hock, Burgundy, and the wines of Bordeaux, especially claret, more generally all feature regularly

in cellar lists, along with port and other fortified wines, such as Malaga, Madeira, sherry, and such dessert wines as Sauternes. Spirits were also drunk, especially whisky (always Scotch), Cognac, and Armagnac.

Downstairs, the major alcoholic drink was beer. In previous centuries, it had been included as part of a servant's allowance. It was also the most common drink served in pubs, which feature in *Downton* as meeting places, and Mr. Bates works in one for a while after his estranged wife, Vera, forces him to leave Downton Abbey. Upper servants sometimes consumed nub ends of wine, and cheap punches were made on special occasions. Ginger beer and mildly alcoholic "pick-me-ups" can be seen at the various fairs, and these were usually home brewed in rural areas, though commercial versions were widely available.

Naturally, coffee and tea were drunk more often than alcoholic drinks, and water more than either of them, especially downstairs. The rich tended to drink seltzer water instead, both for health reasons and because it wasn't associated with poverty (it was also a standard mixer for whiskey). Cordials made from fruit syrup or flavored vinegars were also still in use, especially various fruit "ades," notably lemonade but also orangeade. Pressed juices such as orange juice were rather rarer and, like cocktails, seen as suspiciously un-British.

ANNIE GRAY, *Food Historian*

GLASSWARE

COCKTAIL   COUPE   WINEGLASS   COLLINS   FLUTE   PINT   OLD FASHIONED   MUG   PUNCH BOWL

1

THE LIBRARY

Stirred Drinks &
After-Dinner Drinks

OLD PAL

MAKES **1 COCKTAIL**

In the early 1910s, Scottish-born barman Harry MacElhone was hired by the American-born owner of the New York Bar in Paris to run the operation. A dozen or so years later, he bought the place, renamed it Harry's New York Bar, and made it into a compulsory stop on the itinerary of every well-known American expatriate and international celebrity. MacElhone is credited with creating two interesting Negroni variations that are worth trying. From his 1922 book *ABC of Mixing Cocktails*, the Old Pal dials down the sweetness of a Negroni and kicks up the flavor by using an aged spirit. The cocktail is a great example of how different a cocktail can become with a couple of modifications.
For the second variation, see The Boulevardier on page 28.

1 fl oz (30 ml) rye whiskey or a high-rye Canadian whisky	1 fl oz (30 ml) Campari
1 fl oz (30 ml) dry vermouth	Orange twist, about the size of a thumb, for garnish

Combine all the ingredients in a mixing glass filled with ice and stir until well chilled, 20–30 seconds. Strain into a rocks glass over fresh ice. Express the orange zest over the drink and drop it into the glass.

GRIGG

Will you tell him, or shall I?

CARSON

His name is Charles Grigg. We worked together at one time.

GRIGG

Oh, I'm a little more than that, aren't I, Charlie? We're like brothers, him and me.

CARSON

We're not like brothers.

— SEASON 1, EPISODE 2 —

THE CHEERFUL CHARLIES

MAKES **1 COCKTAIL**

This recipe, a *Downton*-inspired variation on the Old Pal (page 14), is like a great music hall act. It pairs up two different aged spirits for a more complex flavor, and two different liqueurs for less bitterness and more citrus—a combination to get you a standing ovation.

½ fl oz (15 ml) rye whiskey or high-rye Canadian whisky	**1 fl oz (30 ml) dry vermouth**
½ fl oz (15 ml) Cognac	**½ fl oz (15 ml) orange liqueur**
	½ fl oz (15 ml) Campari

Combine all the ingredients in a mixing glass filled with ice and stir until well chilled, 20–30 seconds. Strain into a chilled coupe or cocktail glass.

COUPE

HANKY PANKY

MAKES **1 COCKTAIL**

This cocktail is unique, not just for its use of Fernet, the inky dark and bitter Italian digestif, but also because it was created by Ada "Coley" Coleman, the second-ever female bartender at The Savoy hotel's American Bar in London. She invented the Hanky Panky in the early 1900s for Sir Charles Hawtrey, who asked for something with "a bit of a punch in it." On tasting the cocktail, Hawtrey is reported to have exclaimed, "By Jove! That's the real hanky-panky!"

1½ fl oz (45 ml) gin
1½ fl oz (45 ml) sweet vermouth

2 dashes Fernet-Branca
Orange twist about the size of a thumb, for garnish

Combine the gin, vermouth, and Fernet in a mixing glass filled with ice and stir until well chilled, 20–30 seconds. Strain into a chilled coupe or cocktail glass. Express the orange zest over the drink and drop it into the glass.

— LIBATION NOTE —

The name of the drink most likely came from a simple nonsense rhyme. Such rhymes were a common part of popular culture of the 1920s. Other examples would be hotsy-totsy and the bee's knees, both of which were used to describe something excellent.

COUPE

MARIGOLD

MAKES **1 COCKTAIL**

This Lady Edith inspired variation of the Hanky Panky (page 18), named after her daughter, draws a connection between the pioneering spirit of the original cocktail's creator, Ada Coleman, and the determination of Edith to live as a self-sufficient, modern woman. The Cocchi Americano gives the drink a golden hue, and the addition of lavender bitters harmonizes the botanicals in the gin and Fernet into a springtime garden.

1½ fl oz (45 ml) gin

1½ fl oz (45 ml) Cocchi Americano

2 dashes Fernet-Branca

2 dashes lavender bitters

Orange twist about the size of a thumb, for garnish

Combine the gin, Cocchi Americano, Fernet, and bitters in a mixing glass filled with ice and stir until well chilled, 20–30 seconds. Strain into a chilled coupe or cocktail glass. Express the orange zest over the drink and drop it into the glass.

EDITH

It feels so wild to be out with a man, drinking and dining in a smart London restaurant. Can you imagine being allowed to do anything of the sort five years ago, never mind ten?

— SEASON 4, EPISODE 1 —

COCKTAIL

METROPOLE

MAKES **1 COCKTAIL**

The Hotel Metropole, which once stood at the corner of Forty-second and Broadway in New York City, was well known for its eccentric clientele of bookies and cabaret performers. Essentially a nineteenth-century Cognac martini, the dry, almost-saline Metropole house cocktail is an elegant way to enjoy an old book.

1½ fl oz (45 ml) Cognac

1½ fl oz (45 ml) dry vermouth

2 dashes Creole bitters, such as Peychaud's

Dash orange bitters

2 cherries, for garnish

Combine the Cognac, vermouth, and both bitters in a mixing glass filled with ice and stir until well chilled, 20–30 seconds. Strain into a chilled cocktail glass or coupe. Garnish with the cherries pieced together with a cocktail pick.

> — LIBATION NOTE —
> Swap out the dry vermouth for sweet vermouth and you have a bracing brandy drink for winter nights.

BOSOM CARESSER

MAKES **2 COCKTAILS**

The cocktails of the 1920s often have lurid and evocative names, including this example from the 1921 book *The Whole Art of Dining* by Jean Rey, who commented rather acerbically that "American drinks are nothing but an endless variety of concoctions and mixtures . . . most of them bearing whimsical names by which they are known in Yankee-land." He notes that although Bosom Caresser wasn't a bad name, "it would scarcely be safe in this country to call for such a beverage." Regardless of the name, this is a luxurious cocktail with a decided 1920s kick.

4 fl oz (120 ml) brandy

4 fl oz (120 ml) light cream (see note, page 111)

2 fl oz (60 ml) curaçao or other orange liqueur

1 fl oz (30 ml) raspberry syrup

1 egg yolk

2 orange twists, for garnish

Combine the brandy, cream, curaçao, raspberry syrup, and egg yolk in a shaker. Add ice, shake hard for 8–10 seconds, and strain into 2 collins glasses over ice. Express an orange zest over each drink and drop it into the glass.

— LIBATION NOTE —

The egg yolk adds a lovely texture but can be left out if preferred.

COCKTAIL

LONDON COCKTAIL

MAKES **1 COCKTAIL**

This characteristically heady cocktail is given a frisson of danger by the inclusion of both gin and absinthe, the latter banned in France in 1914 (and in many other countries around the same time). At this point, Absinthe in France was like gin in England in the seventeenth century: widely available, often of dubious quality, highly alcoholic, drunk mainly by the poor, and blamed for everything from epilepsy to murder. Also, just like gin, it originated as a medicine (gin was supposed to cure the plague, and absinthe was used to prevent malaria) and rapidly became popular as a way to get very drunk very quickly. The United Kingdom never banned it (though they had tried to stamp out gin two hundred years previously), so it was still available in London.

½ **barspoon orange bitters**
½ **barspoon simple syrup (see note, page 37)**

½ **barspoon absinthe**
1 fl oz (30 ml) dry gin

Combine all the ingredients in a mixing glass and stir well. Serve in a cocktail or Nick & Nora glass.

DOWNTON ABBEY COCKTAIL BOOK

SHERRY FLIP

MAKES **1 COCKTAIL**

A very old style of drink, flips call for a whole egg (sometimes just the yolk), creating a hearty, fortifying mixture that tastes much better than it sounds. Any of the dry sherries—fino, manzanilla, amontillado—work here.

2½ fl oz (75 ml) dry sherry	**1 egg**
¾ fl oz (20 ml) simple syrup (see note, page 37)	**Ground or freshly grated nutmeg, for garnish**

Combine the sherry, simple syrup, and egg in a shaker. Add ice, shake hard for 8–10 seconds, and strain into a chilled cocktail glass, wineglass, or coupe. Sprinkle with the nutmeg.

— LIBATION NOTE —

You can use a sweeter or heartier sherry here, such as an oloroso, for more intensity, but be sure to dial back the amount of simple syrup (or eliminate it entirely) if you use a cream sherry or anything sweetened.

COCKTAIL

THE BOULEVARDIER

MAKES **1 COCKTAIL**

Like the Old Pal (page 14), this is another Negroni variation from Harry MacElhone's 1927 book *Barflies and Cocktails*. It makes a nice, pleasantly bitter drink—perfect after dinner.

1 fl oz (30 ml) bourbon whiskey

1 fl oz (30 ml) sweet vermouth

1 oz (30 ml) Campari

Orange twist, for garnish

Combine all the ingredients in a mixing glass filled with ice and stir until well chilled, 20–30 seconds. Strain into a chilled cocktail glass. Express the orange zest over the drink and drop it into the glass.

— LIBATION NOTE —

Want to make a Negroni? Simply swap out the whiskey for gin. For a refreshing patio drink, use sparkling wine in place of the hard alcohol.

COUPE

JAPANESE
COCKTAIL

MAKES **1 COCKTAIL**

This recipe is from the 1887 edition of Jerry Thomas's *The Bar-Tenders Guide* and is basically an Old Fashioned (page 146) in a cocktail glass instead of on the rocks. And no, there is nothing Japanese about the drink other than the name.

2 fl oz (60 ml) Cognac	3 dashes Angostura bitters
½ fl oz (15 ml) orgeat syrup	Lemon twist, for garnish

Combine the Cognac, orgeat syrup, and bitters in a mixing glass filled with ice and stir until well chilled, 20–30 seconds. Strain into a chilled coupe or cocktail glass. Express the lemon zest over the drink and drop it into the glass.

MUG

BALTIMORE EGGNOG

MAKES **1 COCKTAIL**

This easy and delicious eggnog, which is basically a flip (see page 27) with milk, requires no cooking and shows up in almost every cocktail book of the mid-1800s in one form or another by the same name. Some recipes require only shaking, but this version from Jerry Thomas's *The Bar-Tender's Guide* calls for separating the egg, beating the white, and then mixing the white into the beaten egg yolk–spirit mixture for a frothy and delightful nog.

1 egg, separated

1½ barspoons rich simple syrup (see note, page 37)

1½ fl oz (45 ml) Cognac brandy or Jamaican rum or a mixture of both

1½ barspoons Madeira or port

4 fl oz (120 ml) whole milk

Whole nutmeg, for garnish

In a small bowl, beat the egg white until stiff peaks form. Set aside.

Combine the egg yolk and simple syrup in a small bowl and beat until blended. Add the Cognac and Madeira and beat until blended. Add the milk and beat again. Finally, add the whipped egg white, beat just until combined, and transfer to a goblet or mug. Grate a little nutmeg on top.

> — LIBATION NOTE —
>
> The foam created by beating the egg white is worth the effort, but if you're feeling lazy, just shake all the ingredients in a shaker.

TUXEDO
COCKTAIL № 2

MAKES **1 COCKTAIL**

This cocktail is basically a dry martini dressed up with the addition of maraschino liqueur and absinthe. A smart suit or dress can change the way we think of a person, and in that same way, those minor additions shift the cocktail toward elegant.

1½ fl oz (45 ml) Old Tom gin

1 fl oz (30 ml) dry vermouth

½ barspoon maraschino liqueur

¼ barspoon absinthe

2 dashes orange bitters

Cherry and lemon twist, for garnish

Combine the gin, vermouth, maraschino liqueur, absinthe, and bitters in a mixing glass filled with ice and stir until well chilled, 20–30 seconds. Strain into a chilled cocktail glass or coupe. Garnish with the cherry, putting it directly into the glass, and then express the lemon zest over the drink and drop it into the glass.

> **— LIBATION NOTE —**
>
> The small amount of absinthe makes a surprising difference to the flavor of the cocktail. Add a little more than the couple of dashes called for and the drink will take on a strong black licorice taste that will throw the drink off balance.

ISOBEL
We've asked Molesley to look at Matthew's old morning coat. He's confident he can make it fit.

BRANSON
That's very kind, ladies, but, you see, I don't approve of these costumes. I see them as the uniform of oppression, and I should be uncomfortable wearing them.

VIOLET
Are you quite finished?

BRANSON
I have.

VIOLET
Good. Please take off your coat.

— SEASON 3, EPISODE 1 —

MORNING COAT

MAKES **1 COCKTAIL**

Tom Branson's initiation to life upstairs in the Grantham household
required some adjustments by both sides. The morning coat was the first
step of many that changed Tom and family forever. In this variation
on the Tuxedo Cocktail No. 2 (page 32), the dry vermouth gets replaced
by Cocchi Americano, for a less herbal and more citrusy drink.

1½ fl oz (45 ml) Irish whiskey

**1 fl oz (30 ml) Cocchi Americano
or other Kina Lillet–style aperitif**

½ barspoon maraschino liqueur

¼ barspoon absinthe

2 dashes orange bitters

**Cherry and lemon twist,
for garnish**

Combine the whiskey, Cocchi Americano, maraschino liqueur, absinthe, and
bitters in a mixing glass filled with ice and stir until well chilled, 20–30 seconds.
Strain into a chilled cocktail glass or coupe. Garnish with the cherry, putting
it directly into the glass, and then express the lemon zest over the drink and
drop it into the glass.

– LIBATION NOTE –

If Tom Branson were making this drink, he'd be sure to use a whiskey
made in the Republic of Ireland rather than one made in Northern
Ireland. Flavorwise, the light blended style of whiskey from either location
will work. Kina Lillet was a late-nineteenth-century French wine–based
aperitif with quinine and other botanicals. It has been out of production
since the mid-twentieth century. Cocchi Americano works best as a modern-day substitute, but Salers or Kina l'Avion d'Or can also be used.

IMPROVED BRANDY COCKTAIL

MAKES **1 COCKTAIL**

In the late 1800s, absinthe started showing up in many drinks, including in old ones billed as improved versions. The spirit's long list of botanicals usually includes anise, which gives it a sensation of sweetness that helps round out cocktails without the addition of sugar.

2 fl oz (60 ml) Cognac

2 dashes Boker's or Angostura bitters

½ barspoon maraschino liqueur

1 barspoon gum syrup

⅛ barspoon absinthe

Lemon twist, for garnish

Combine the Cognac, bitters, maraschino liqueur, gum syrup, and absinthe in a mixing glass filled with ice and stir until well chilled, 20–30 seconds. Strain into a chilled cocktail glass or coupe. Express the lemon zest over the drink and drop it into the glass.

— LIBATION NOTE —

Gum syrup is a rich simple syrup, which means it has a ratio of two parts sugar to one part water, with the addition of gum arabic. The gum arabic is an edible stabilizer and thickener, bestowing a velvety richness to cocktails.

COFFEE COCKTAIL

MAKES **1 COCKTAIL**

This recipe, which originally appeared in Alfred Suzanne's 1904 book *La Cuisine et pâtisserie anglaise et américaine*, is a great way to have your after-dinner drink and coffee at the same time. It also makes for a potent brunch drink—think of it as a creamy coffee julep.

2 fl oz (60 ml) brewed espresso, at room temperature

2 fl oz (60 ml) brandy

2 fl oz (60 ml) heavy cream

1½ barspoons simple syrup (see note)

6 barspoons crushed ice

Ground or freshly grated nutmeg, for garnish

Combine the espresso, brandy, cream, simple syrup, and crushed ice in a shaker and shake hard for 8–10 seconds. Pour the whole mixture, ice and all, into a collins glass and sprinkle with the nutmeg. Serve with a straw.

— **LIBATION NOTE** —

To make simple syrup, combine equal parts sugar and water in a saucepan and heat, stirring, until the sugar fully dissolves. For rich simple syrup, use two parts sugar to one part water. Simple syrup will keep for 3–4 weeks in a tightly lidded jar in the refrigerator; rich simple syrup, stored the same way, will keep for up to 4 months.

2

THE GROUNDS

Refreshing Drinks

COUPE

SIDECAR

MAKES **1 COCKTAIL**

This is one of those drinks whose origin and name are locked in disagreement, with many claiming it came from the Paris Ritz, and others that it came about when someone drove a motorcycle into a Paris bistro soon after World War I. Old recipes from such books as the 1927 edition of *Barflies and Cocktails* call for all three ingredients in equal proportions, which makes for a shockingly tart and sweet drink. This recipe uses the more modern proportions of a sour, but if you feel the need to taste the original, by all means try it.

Lemon wedge, for rimming
Sugar, for rimming
2 fl oz (60 ml) brandy

¾ fl oz (20 ml) orange liqueur
¾ fl oz (20 ml) fresh lemon juice

Run the lemon wedge along the rim of a chilled coupe or cocktail glass. Pour a small mound of sugar onto a flat saucer. Tip the glass so it is almost parallel to the plate and gently roll its dampened edge in the sugar to create a sugar-frosted rim.

Combine the brandy, orange liqueur, and lemon juice in a shaker. Add ice, shake hard for 8–10 seconds, and strain into the prepared glass.

COUPE

THE SUFFRAGETTE

MAKES **1 COCKTAIL**

The most progressive of the three sisters, Lady Sybil made choices that often shocked the family, from her support of women's right to vote to her work as a nurse during the war. But none surprised them as much as her love of Tom Branson, the chauffeur. This adaptation of the Sidecar (page 43) is on the sweeter side.

Lemon wedge, for rimming	**2 fl oz (60 ml) brandy**
Granulated or superfine sugar, for rimming	**¾ fl oz (20 ml) crème de cacao**
	¾ fl oz (20 ml) fresh lemon juice

Run the lemon wedge along the rim of a chilled coupe or cocktail glass. Pour a small mound of sugar onto a flat saucer. Tip the glass so it is almost parallel to the plate and gently roll its dampened edge in the sugar to create a sugar-frosted rim.

Combine the brandy, crème de cacao, and lemon juice in a shaker. Add ice, shake hard for 8–10 seconds, and strain into the prepared glass.

― LIBATION NOTE ―

Use a good-quality crème de cacao, which will add a slight cocoa bitterness and real chocolate flavor.

BRANSON

The truth is, I'll stay in Downton until you want to run away with me.

SYBIL

Don't be ridiculous.

BRANSON

You're too scared to admit it but you're in love with me.

— SEASON 2, EPISODE 3 —

RASPBERRY GIN FIZZ

COLLINS

MAKES **1 COCKTAIL**

The fizz is a style of drink that utilizes the effervescence of club soda or seltzer water to give levity and refreshing qualities and includes siblings like the Ramos Gin Fizz (see right), Morning Glory Fizz (page 108), Gin Rickey (page 118), and countless other variations. This version gets dressed up with raspberry syrup, a popular addition in the late nineteenth century.

2 fl oz (60 ml) Old Tom gin
¾ fl oz (20 ml) fresh lime juice
¾ fl oz (20 ml) raspberry syrup

5–6 fl oz (150–180 ml) club soda, chilled
Lime wedge and raspberries, for garnish

Combine the gin, lime juice, and raspberry syrup in a shaker. Add ice, shake hard for 8–10 seconds, and strain into a chilled collins glass. Add the club soda and stir briefly, then add as many ice cubes as will fit without spilling. Garnish with the lime wedge and raspberries.

> **— LIBATION NOTE —**
> Popular in eighteenth-century England, Old Tom is a style of gin that is slightly sweet. It got its name from signs shaped like a black cat (an "old tom") displayed on pubs to signify the gin was served there.

WINEGLASS

RAMOS GIN FIZZ

MAKES **1 COCKTAIL**

Although this is the most famous fizz, it is actually not a true fizz because it departs from both the classic ingredients and construction method (see left). The secret of this drink, created in the late nineteenth century by New Orleans restaurateur Henry Ramos, lies in the shaking: a full three minutes. That's a long time, but some feel it is the only way to achieve the trademark silky mouthfeel. Feel free to shake it as long as you can.

2 fl oz (60 ml) gin

½ fl oz (15 ml) fresh lime juice

½ fl oz (15 ml) fresh lemon juice

½ fl oz (15 ml) simple syrup (see note, page 37)

4 drops orange flower water

1 egg white

1 fl oz (30 ml) light cream (see note, page 111)

2 fl oz (60 ml) club soda

Combine the gin, citrus juices, simple syrup, orange flower water, egg white, and cream in a shaker. Add ice and shake hard for 3 minutes—or for as long as you can. Strain into a chilled wineglass or collins glass. Add the club soda and stir briefly.

— LIBATION NOTE —

If you double strain the drink by pouring it through a tea strainer or small fine-mesh sieve on its way into the glass, you will get finer bubbles and better texture in the drink.

COCKTAIL

THE ABBEY

MAKES **1 COCKTAIL**

This recipe, which comes from *The Savoy Cocktail Book*, is a great cocktail for using gins with more unusual botanicals, like citrus or floral components, but it works perfectly fine with standard London Dry, too. Topping it with a float of Champagne wouldn't hurt if you are serving guests at brunch, or even dinner.

1½ fl oz (45 ml) gin
¾ fl oz (20 ml) Cocchi Americano

¾ fl oz (20 ml) fresh orange juice

Combine all the ingredients in a shaker. Add ice, shake hard for 8–10 seconds, and strain into a chilled cocktail glass or coupe.

LIBATION NOTE
As in any cocktail with orange juice, use fresh-squeezed or high-quality bottled juice or the drink will taste flat. Sometimes the addition of a few drops of lemon juice will help liven it up.

LIBATION NOTE

Since the orange juice was traded out for vermouth, the drink should be stirred and not shaken. The general rule for shaking versus stirring is this: If there is juice, dairy, or egg, you shake it. Otherwise, stir it. There are, of course, always exceptions, like highball drinks that are "built" in a serving glass can include juice but are not shaken. They often benefit from a quick stir, too.

COCKTAIL

DOWNTON HEIR

MAKES **1 COCKTAIL**

The sudden death of Robert's heir on the *Titanic* catapults Matthew from Manchester lawyer to reluctant heir to the title of earl and the Downton estate. Taking The Abbey cocktail (page 48) and twisting it to be a more elegant fifty-fifty gin martini seems an appropriate tribute.

1½ fl oz (45 ml) gin
¾ fl oz (20 ml) Cocchi Americano

¾ fl oz (20 ml) dry vermouth

Combine all the ingredients in a mixing glass filled with ice and stir until well chilled, 20–30 seconds. Strain into a chilled cocktail glass or coupe.

MATTHEW
I've got a job in Ripon. I've said I'll start tomorrow.

ROBERT
A job? You do know I mean to involve you in the running of the estate.

MATTHEW
Don't worry. There are plenty of hours in the day. And, of course, I'll have the weekend.

VIOLET
What is a weekend?

— SEASON 1, EPISODE 2 —

SUMMER CUP

MAKES **1 COCKTAIL**

Also called a Pimm's Cup, this marvellously refreshing long drink was created in the 1820s by Londoner James Pimm at his restaurant. Starting from traditional English fruit cups, which were a mix of fruit, juices, spirits, and sugar, Pimm concocted a gin-based tonic, flavored with fruit liqueurs and herbs, and began selling it commercially in 1859. The company eventually developed six varieties of Pimm's, each using a different spirit—gin, scotch, brandy, rum, vodka, rye whiskey—though most of them are no longer available.

2 fl oz (60 ml) Pimm's No. 1
4 fl oz (120 ml) ginger ale

Ribbon of cucumber and orange wheel (optional), for garnish

In an ice-filled collins glass, combine the Pimm's and ginger ale and stir to mix. Garnish with the cucumber ribbon and orange wheel (if using).

LIBATION NOTE

Summer cups can be
decorated with as many
kinds of fruit as you like,
each adding color to the
drink. To make something
special, try layering the
fruit: add some ice, then
fruit, then more ice, and so
on, until you end up with
garnish strata.

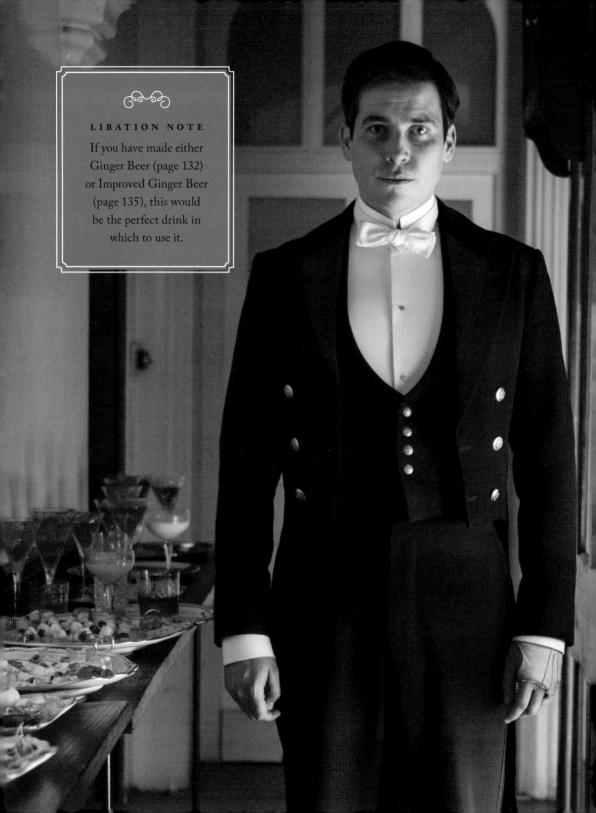

LIBATION NOTE

If you have made either
Ginger Beer (page 132)
or Improved Ginger Beer
(page 135), this would
be the perfect drink in
which to use it.

COLLINS

SUB-ROSA SUMMER

MAKES **1 COCKTAIL**

Replacing the mild ginger ale of the Summer Cup (page 52) with ginger beer adds the necessary bite that's as spicy as Barrow's wrath. Barrow would probably drink this alone, but we suggest you share it with a friend.

2 fl oz (60 ml) Pimm's No. 1
4 fl oz (120 ml) ginger beer

Ribbon of cucumber and orange wheel, for garnish
2 dashes Peychaud's bitters

In an ice-filled collins glass, combine the Pimm's and ginger beer and stir to mix. Garnish with the cucumber ribbon and orange wheel. Top with the bitters.

CROWBOROUGH
I remember this man. You served me when I dined with Lady Grantham in London.

THOMAS
I did, Your Grace.

CROWBOROUGH
Ah, there we are. We shall do very well together, won't we . . . ?

THOMAS
Thomas, Your Grace.

CROWBOROUGH
Thomas. Good.

— SEASON 1, EPISODE 1 —

GREEN SWIZZLE

MAKES **1 COCKTAIL**

Invented in the late 1800s, this Caribbean-born drink gets its name from the wooden tool that, when submerged in the drink and quickly spun back and forth between your palms, makes the drink frothy. If you don't have a swizzle stick, stir the drink with a barspoon and it will still taste good.

1½ fl oz (45 ml) white rum
¾ fl oz (20 ml) falernum
¾ fl oz (20 ml) fresh lime juice

1 barspoon absinthe
Dash Angostura bitters

Combine the rum, falernum, lime juice, and absinthe in a collins glass and fill halfway with crushed ice. Whip vigorously with a swizzle stick to combine. Add more crushed ice to fill and finish with the bitters on top for color. Serve with a straw.

— **LIBATION NOTE** —

The bitters will give you plenty of blood-red color on top, but the color of the drink itself will depend on your choice of absinthe, which can range from neon green (food coloring) to almost brown (natural color). Good-quality absinthe should be a nice vegetal brown.

COUPE

DAIQUIRI

MAKES **1 COCKTAIL**

Named for an area near the Cuban city of Santiago de Cuba, the daiquiri became popular after the recipe was introduced in 1909 at the Army and Navy Club in Washington, DC, by a junior medical officer, Lucius W. Johnson. Originally built in a collins glass and stirred, the daiquiri evolved into a shaken drink, but there's nothing wrong with having this over ice if the weather demands it.

2 fl oz (60 ml) white rum
¾ fl oz (20 ml) fresh lime juice

¾ fl oz (20 ml) simple syrup (see note, page 37)
Lime wheel, for garnish

Combine the rum, lime juice, and simple syrup in a shaker. Add ice, shake hard for 8–10 seconds, and strain into a chilled coupe or cocktail glass. Garnish with the lime wheel.

– LIBATION NOTE –

The daiquiri belongs to the family of mixed drinks known as sours or sour cocktails. Sours are some of the most popular libations, with a bloodline filled with such royalty as the Sidecar (page 43) and even the White Lady (page 103). You'd think that a recipe that calls for only three ingredients would be boring, but swap out the rum for tequila and you have a margarita, or trade it out for gin and you have a gimlet!

COUPE

CLOVER CLUB

MAKES **1 COCKTAIL**

Developed by barman George Boldt, who owned Philadelphia's Bellevue-Stratford Hotel on South Broad Street, this frothy and delicate drink is named for a local men's club that met regularly at the hotel from the late 1800s to the early 1900s.

1 fl oz (30 ml) gin
1 fl oz (30 ml) dry vermouth
½ fl oz (15 ml) fresh lemon juice

½ fl oz (15 ml) egg white (about ½ egg white)
½ fl oz (15 ml) raspberry syrup
1½ barspoons simple syrup (see note, page 37)

Combine all the ingredients in a shaker and shake hard for 10–15 seconds so the egg white froths up and emulsifies. Fill the shaker with ice, re-cover, and shake hard for about 10 seconds longer. Strain into a chilled coupe glass.

— LIBATION NOTE —

Although this drink doesn't traditionally come with more than its frothy head as a garnish, try it with a mint sprig, slapped between your hands in a clapping motion to release the aroma before dropping it into the glass.

OLD FASHIONED

MINT JULEP

MAKES **1 COCKTAIL**

Basically a whiskey sling (a drink with spirits, sugar, and water) with crushed ice instead of water, this is the drink that launched mixology. Simple, elegant, and, most importantly, cold, it comes with an aromatic mint garnish that one inhales as one sips the sweetened bourbon.

¾ fl oz (20 ml) simple syrup (see note, page 37)

2 fl oz (60 ml) bourbon whiskey

3 large mint sprigs, for garnish

Pour the simple syrup into a julep cup or old fashioned glass filled with crushed ice. Stir well. Add the bourbon and stir until a film of ice forms on the exterior of the cup. Garnish with the mint sprigs.

─ **LIBATION NOTE** ─

Juleps can be made with spirits other than bourbon. In fact, peach brandy was the earlier basis for the drink, but your favorite spirit—gin, Cognac, and even fortified wines like sherry and port—will work here, too.

COLLINS

JOHN COLLINS

MAKES **1 COCKTAIL**

Legend has it that this drink was named for a waiter named John Collins,
who worked at a London restaurant called Limmer's. It was first recorded
in cocktail books in the late nineteenth century, and some early recipes
called for whiskey rather than gin.

2 fl oz (60 ml) genever
½ fl oz (15 ml) fresh lemon juice
**½ fl oz (15 ml) simple syrup
(see note, page 37)**

5–6 fl oz (150–180 ml) club soda
Lemon wedge, for garnish

Combine the genever, lemon juice, and simple syrup in a shaker. Add ice,
shake hard for 8–10 seconds, and strain into a collins glass filled with ice.
Pour in the club soda and stir briefly. Garnish with the lemon wedge.

— **LIBATION NOTE** —

Genever is an old Dutch-style gin that inspired English adaptations like
Old Tom, London Dry, and Plymouth. It is traditionally distilled from a
mixture of botanicals that include juniper, and it is sweetened with a malt
wine. The taste is something of a mix between whiskey and gin, which
gives drinks a lively fresh bread flavor. Using whiskey here isn't that big
of a leap from genever.

COUPE

DAISY

MAKES **1 COCKTAIL**

A category of cocktail popular around the late 1800s, the Daisy was simply a sour cocktail with the addition of a small amount of seltzer water. Not to be confused with a fizz, which features three to four times the amount of soda water, the daisy has just enough seltzer to let the drink bloom.

2 fl oz (60 ml) Cognac
½ fl oz (15 ml) fresh lemon juice
1 barspoon orange liqueur

1 barspoon gum syrup (see note, page 36)
About 1 fl oz (30 ml) seltzer water

Combine the Cognac, lemon juice, orange liqueur, and gum syrup in a shaker. Add ice, shake hard for 8–10 seconds, and strain into a chilled coupe or cocktail glass. Top with the seltzer.

— LIBATION NOTE —
A barspoon is equivalent to 1 teaspoon (5 ml), in case you don't have a standard one in your bar.

COUPE

MASON DAISY

MAKES **1 COCKTAIL**

A twist on the classic Daisy (page 63), this version swaps out the seltzer for cider, something that Mr. Mason makes on his farm. A few dashes of bitters for Daisy's crushes on Alfred and Thomas add a little spice to complement the ginger.

2 fl oz (60 ml) Cognac
½ fl oz (15 ml) fresh lemon juice
1 barspoon orange liqueur

1 barspoon gum syrup
(see note, page 36)
2 dashes Angostura bitters
About 1 fl oz (30 ml) cider
or ginger beer

Combine the Cognac, lemon juice, orange liqueur, gum syrup, and bitters in a shaker. Add ice, shake hard for 8–10 seconds, and strain into a chilled coupe or cocktail glass. Top with the ginger beer.

DAISY
I've never been special to anyone.

MASON
Except William.

DAISY
That's right. I were only ever special to William. I never thought of it like that before.

MASON
Well, now you're special to me.

— SEASON 2, EPISODE 9 —

THE GROUNDS

CHAMPAGNE COBBLER

MAKES **1 COCKTAIL**

Cobblers are a style of drink from the mid-1800s that were designed, like juleps (see Mint Julep, page 60), to cool you down in a hurry. But unlike juleps, the ice here isn't flaky and snowy. It is instead crushed to the size of small pebbles, or "cobbles."

½ fl oz (15 ml) rich simple syrup or gum syrup (see notes, pages 37 and 36, respectively)

Sparkling wine (preferably brut)

Lemon twist and orange twist, for garnish

Mixed seasonal berries or other fruit, for garnish

Pour the simple syrup into a julep cup or double old fashioned glass filled two-thirds full with pebble-size ice. Add the sparkling wine to the cup to fill. Express the citrus zests over the drink and drop them into the cup. Garnish with the berries. Serve with a straw.

— LIBATION NOTE —

You can swap out the rich simple syrup for raspberry syrup, which will accentuate the berry garnish but not dominate the drink.

COUPE

LAST WORD

MAKES **1 COCKTAIL**

This pre-Prohibition cocktail first developed at the Detroit Athletic Club is a bumblebee of the bar world: by all calculations, it shouldn't fly, yet it does. Balanced and herbal, but not too herbal; sweet enough to balance the lime juice, but not too sweet—it makes a great nightcap.

¾ fl oz (20 ml) gin
¾ fl oz (20 ml) maraschino liqueur

¾ fl oz (20 ml) green Chartreuse
¾ fl oz (20 ml) fresh lime juice
Lime wheel, for garnish

Combine the gin, maraschino liqueur, Chartreuse, and lime juice in a shaker. Add ice, shake hard for 8–10 seconds, and strain into a chilled coupe or cocktail glass. Garnish with the lime wheel.

VIOLET
*It makes me smile the way every year we drink
to the future whatever it may bring.*

ISOBEL
*Well what else could we drink to?
We're going forward to the future not back into the past.*

VIOLET
If only we had the choice.

— SEASON 6, EPISODE 9 —

LIBATION NOTE

Crème de violet is a liqueur
version of violet candies,
with a floral sweetness that
turns this drink into a purple
and powerful potentate.

COUPE

FINAL SAY

MAKES **1 COCKTAIL**

Do not cross Violet, matriarch of the Crawley family, whose skill at disarming opponents and getting what she wants is supreme. Like the Dowager Countess of Grantham, do not underestimate this cocktail, a riff on the Last Word (page 68). It may read like drinking a floral arrangement, but it's both potent and balanced.

¾ fl oz (20 ml) gin

¾ fl oz (20 ml) maraschino liqueur

¾ fl oz (20 ml) crème de violet

¾ fl oz (20 ml) fresh lime juice

Lime wheel, for garnish

Combine the gin, maraschino liqueur, crème de violet, and lime juice in a shaker. Add ice, shake hard for 8–10 seconds, and strain into a chilled coupe or cocktail glass. Garnish with the lime wheel.

CORA
I wish I could remind your mother we're on the same side.

ROBERT
I doubt it—when it comes to sides Mother is a law unto herself.

– SEASON 6, EPISODE 2 –

NEW YORK SOUR

MAKES **1 COCKTAIL**

Essentially a wine-topped whiskey daisy—the daisy being a sour topped with seltzer—the New York sour is an elegant drink that would work well with hors d'oeuvres. Note that claret is an old British term for red wines from Bordeaux, but any nice fruity red wine will work here.

2 fl oz (60 ml) whiskey

¾ fl oz (20 ml) simple syrup (see note, page 37)

¾ fl oz (20 ml) fresh lemon juice

About ¾ fl oz (20 ml) seltzer water

About 1 fl oz (30 ml) claret

Combine the whiskey, simple syrup, and lemon juice in a shaker. Add ice, shake hard for 8–10 seconds, and strain into a chilled cocktail glass. Top with the seltzer, then float with the claret, poured carefully on the back of the spoon to create a red layer (see note).

— **LIBATION NOTE** —

The trick to floating—or layering—a liquor, wine, or other ingredient on top of a drink is easier than it looks, and all you need is a barspoon. Place the barspoon on the surface of the drink so the convex side sticks up, like a little metal island, then slowly pour the liquid onto the spoon. Because the claret in this sour is less dense than the cocktail, it will float as a separate layer.

LADY'S MAID

MAKES **1 COCKTAIL**

In the series, Cora's lady's maids, Baxter and O'Brien, are polar opposites, and this drink plays on those personalities through the New York Sour (page 75): it can be made sweet or bitter.

2 fl oz (60 ml) whiskey

½ fl oz (15 ml) simple syrup (see note, page 37)

¾ fl oz (20 ml) fresh lemon juice

About ¾ fl oz (20 ml) seltzer water

½ fl oz (15 ml) ruby port for Baxter version, or Campari or other similar Italian-style aperitif liqueur, for O'Brien version

Combine the whiskey, simple syrup, and lemon juice in a shaker. Add ice, shake hard for 8–10 seconds, and strain into a chilled coupe or cocktail glass. Top with the seltzer, then float with the port, for a Baxter version, or with the Campari, for an O'Brien version (see note, page 75).

─ **LIBATION NOTE** ─

The floats aren't really floats here, as their sugar content will make them sink to the bottom of the drink, creating a layer that will make the drink either slightly sweeter (in the Baxter version) or more bitter (in the O'Brien).

LIBATION NOTE

This punch is ideal for scaling down to serve just a few people as a nightcap or at the start of a party, and it can be made in a microwave in individual mugs. For a small mug, try just over 1 fl oz (30 ml) each of brandy and rum, sugar to taste, a pinch of each of the spices, and an orange slice, heat it all up, and top with a little hot strong black tea.

TEA PUNCH

SERVES **6–8**

Hot punches like this one were winter drinks, served at balls and at holiday celebrations such as Christmas and New Year's. The original title of the recipe was *Punch au thé à l'anglaise*, pointing out, once again, the association of the English with black tea. It comes from Alfred Suzanne's 1904 book *La Cuisine et pâtisserie anglaise et américaine*, which was aimed at French chefs aspiring to work in the United Kingdom or the United States. It purported to contain all the recipes that each nation regarded as a necessity on its tables. It was an odd claim, since in the author's view there really was no need for any type of food that wasn't French. For an added flourish, hang orange peel strips over the edge of the punch bowl.

1⅔ cups (385 ml) aged rum
1⅔ cups (385 ml) brandy
¼ cup (50 g) sugar
Zest of ½ lemon, cut into strips

¼ teaspoon ground cinnamon, or ½ cinnamon stick
¼ teaspoon ground cloves, or 6 whole cloves
2¼ cups (525 ml) hot strong black tea
8 orange slices

Combine the rum, brandy, sugar, lemon zest, cinnamon, and cloves in a saucepan over medium-high heat and heat until just below boiling, stirring to dissolve the sugar. Pour the hot mixture into a heatproof punch bowl or other serving vessel. Add the hot tea and orange slices and stir briefly. Serve immediately in heatproof glasses, small mugs, or punch cups.

GHILLIES JUICE

MAKES **1 COCKTAIL**

So yes, this recipe is really for laughs and a riff on Tea Punch (page 79) in honor of Mr. Molesley. Interestingly enough, however, it is thought that it was the desire to create one glass of punch at a time for a customer that evolved into the modern-day cocktail. England mastered the punch bowl over centuries, but it was the availability of ice extracted from frozen ponds and various storage techniques that together ensured ice would be available year-round, allowing bartenders in the United States to popularize and evolve cocktails. Enterprising Europeans and ex-pat Americans imported the idea, opening up "American bars" across the continent that showcased American bartenders during Prohibition.

1 fl oz (30 ml) whiskey	**1 cup (240 ml) Tea Punch (page 79)**

Put on your dancing shoes and hide your car keys. Add the whiskey to the punch and drink. Dance wildly.

ROBERT

They do say there's a wild man inside all of us.

VIOLET

If only he would stay inside.

— SEASON 3, EPISODE 9 —

LIBATION NOTE

Be careful with the
number of these fortified
cups of punch you drink.
On second thought, maybe
you should stick to
Tea Punch.

BRANDY CRUSTA

MAKES **1 COCKTAIL**

Perfected in New Orleans in the 1850s, this drink was not known outside of the area until Jerry Thomas included it in his 1887 edition of *The Bar-Tender's Guide*. The look of the drink, with a coil of lemon zest nested in the glass and a rim frosted with sugar, made it as irresistible then as it is today.

Lemon wedge, for rimming, plus 1 lemon	1 barspoon fresh lemon juice
Sugar, for rimming	1 barspoon gum syrup (see note, page 36)
2 fl oz (60 ml) brandy	2 dashes Angostura bitters or other aromatic bitters
½ barspoon orange liqueur	

Run the lemon wedge along the rim of a chilled wineglass or coupe. Pour a small mound of sugar onto a flat saucer. Tip the glass so it is almost parallel to the plate and gently roll its dampened edge in the sugar to create a sugar-frosted rim.

Using a vegetable peeler, cut the zest from the whole lemon in a continuous wide strip, coil the strip, and slip it into the prepared glass. It will uncoil to almost fill the glass. This is a horse's neck twist (see note, page 84). Set aside.

Combine the brandy, orange liqueur, lemon juice, gum syrup, and bitters in a shaker. Add ice, shake for 8–10 seconds, and strain into the prepared glass.

TURKISH ATTACHÉ

MAKES **1 COCKTAIL**

No other scandal in the series threatens ruin for Lady Mary or looms quite as ominously as the death of Kemal Pamuk. And yet, no one else could have dealt with the scandal as elegantly as Mary. A variation on the Brandy Crusta (see left), this drink, like that scandal, will quietly disappear in your glass.

Lemon wedge, for rimming, plus 1 lemon

Sugar, for rimming

2 fl oz (60 ml) brandy

½ fl oz (15 ml) velvet falernum liqueur

¾ oz (20 ml) fresh lemon juice

1 barspoon passion fruit syrup

4 dashes Angostura or other aromatic bitters

Run the lemon wedge along the rim of a chilled coupe or wineglass. Pour a small mound of sugar onto a flat saucer. Tip the glass so it is almost parallel to the plate and gently roll its dampened edge in the sugar to create a sugar-frosted rim.

Using a vegetable peeler, cut the zest from the whole lemon in a continuous wide strip, coil the strip, and slip it into the prepared glass. It will uncoil to almost fill the interior—like a bedsheet. This is a horse's neck twist (see note, page 84).

Combine the brandy, velvet falernum, lemon juice, passion fruit syrup, and bitters in a shaker. Add ice, shake for 8–10 seconds, and strain into the prepared glass.

> — LIBATION NOTE —
>
> A surprising ingredient that shows up in a lot of old cocktail recipes, passion fruit syrup (or "pash") makes this drink both exotic and exciting.

LIBATION NOTE

To make a horse's neck twist, pick a lemon with a relatively thick rind so you don't crush the fruit as you remove the zest. A vegetable peeler usually works best, but a paring or canelle (channel) knife can also be used. Cut the zest from the whole lemon in a continuous long, wide strip. Coil the strip into a tight spiral and carefully slide it into the glass, where it will unwind, almost filling the interior.

TURKISH ATTACHÉ
see recipe, page 83

VIOLET

*Oh, my dears. Is it really true? I can't believe it. Last night he looked
so well. Of course, it would happen to a foreigner. It's typical.*

MARY

Don't be ridiculous.

VIOLET

*I'm not being ridiculous. No Englishman would dream of dying in
someone else's house—especially somebody they didn't even know.*

— SEASON 1, EPISODE 3 —

PRINCE OF WALES COCKTAIL

MAKES **1 COCKTAIL**

Although it shares the same name as the punch on page 102, this cocktail is reputed to have been invented by Prince Albert Edward himself. It comes from a 1901 book titled *The Private Life of King Edward VII*.

1½ fl oz (45 ml) rye whiskey or a high-rye Canadian whisky

1½ barspoons rich simple syrup (see note, page 37)

¼ barspoon maraschino liqueur

Dash Angostura bitters

Thumb-size chunk pineapple

1½ fl oz (45 ml) sparkling wine (preferably brut)

Lemon twist, for garnish

Combine the whiskey, simple syrup, maraschino liqueur, bitters, and pineapple in a shaker. Add ice, shake hard for 8–10 seconds, and strain into a chilled coupe or cocktail glass. Float the sparkling wine on top (see note, page 75). Express the lemon zest over the drink and drop it into the glass.

> **— LIBATION NOTE —**
>
> The chunk of pineapple will get smashed up during the shaking of the drink, so there's no need to muddle the fruit, but you will end up with a lot of pulp in your shaker. To make a drink fit for a prince, double strain it by pouring it through a tea strainer or small fine-mesh sieve on its way into the glass.

THE GREAT HALL

COUPE

WILD ROSE

MAKES **1 COCKTAIL**

Rebellious and fun-loving Lady Rose needs a cocktail that balances her wild and experimental side with her traditional one. This drink, based on the Prince of Wales Cocktail (page 87)—she danced with the prince at her debutante ball—calls for tequila, a spirit known but not common in 1920s England. It is a liquor from the Americas, where Rose moves to after marrying Atticus.

1½ fl oz (45 ml) reposado tequila	Thumb-size chunk pineapple
1½ barspoons rich simple syrup (see note, page 37)	1½ fl oz (45 ml) sparkling wine (preferably brut)
¼ barspoon maraschino liqueur	Orange twist rose, for garnish (see note)
Dash Angostura bitters	

Combine the tequila, simple syrup, maraschino liqueur, bitters, and pineapple in a shaker. Add ice, shake hard for 8–10 seconds, and strain into a chilled coupe or cocktail glass. Float the sparkling wine on top (see note, page 75), then garnish with the orange twist rose.

— LIBATION NOTE —

An orange twist rose is pretty and easy to make: wind a medium-width but long strip of orange zest into itself and skewer it with a cocktail pick to keep it from unwinding.

ROSE
*Oh, by the way, Madeleine Allsopp asked if I'd go on to the Embassy
with some friends of hers, afterwards.*

ROBERT
Tonight? After the dinner?

CORA
Rose, once you get past Tuesday . . .

ROSE
*I don't think you have to be presented to go to the Embassy Club.
And I do love Ambrose and his orchestra. Please.*

MARY
Your niece is a flapper. Accept it.

ROSE
I'm not a flapper. But can I go?

— SEASON 4, EPISODE 9 —

FLUTE

FRENCH 75

MAKES **1 COCKTAIL**

Created around the time of World War I, this elegant drink was said to pack the wallop of a 75mm French artillery shell, thus its name.

1½ fl oz (45 ml) gin

½ fl oz (15 ml) fresh lemon juice

½ fl oz (15 ml) simple syrup
(see note, page 37)

3 dashes orange bitters

2 lemon zest strips

About 2 fl oz (60 ml) brut
sparkling wine, chilled

Combine the gin, lemon juice, simple syrup, bitters, and 1 zest strip in a shaker. Add ice, shake hard for 8–10 seconds, and strain into a chilled champagne flute or coupe. Top with the sparkling wine. Express the remaining zest strip over the drink and drop it into the glass.

— LIBATION NOTE —

Shaking the lemon zest with the other ingredients can make the drink a little bitter, so if you want a bit less intensity, leave it out.

FLUTE

ARCHIE'S MEMORIAL

MAKES **1 COCKTAIL**

If Mrs. Patmore were a bartender, she would have created a drink to honor her nephew, Archie Philpotts, who died in the war but was left out of his town's memorial. This slight twist on a French 75 (page 91) gets the subtle but meaningful addition of sage leaves, which gives it a citrusy herbal hint.

1½ fl oz (45 ml) gin

½ fl oz (15 ml) fresh lemon juice

½ fl oz (15 ml) simple syrup (see note, page 37)

2 dashes orange bitters

4 fresh sage leaves

About 2 fl oz (60 ml) brut sparkling wine, chilled

Lemon twist, for garnish

Combine the gin, lemon juice, simple syrup, bitters, and sage leaves in a shaker. Add ice, shake hard for 8–10 seconds, and strain into a chilled champagne flute or coupe. Top with the sparkling wine. Express the lemon zest over the drink and drop it into the glass.

— LIBATION NOTE —

It wouldn't be a drink from Mrs. Patmore if it didn't include food. By design, this drink goes very well with a nice piece of Cheddar cheese.

KIR ROYAL

MAKES **1 COCKTAIL**

This iconic French cocktail was named for a certain Canon Félix Kir, once mayor of Dijon, France, a city that produces crème de cassis from local black currants.

5 fl oz (150 ml) Champagne or sparkling wine, chilled

2 barspoons crème de cassis
Lemon twist, for garnish

Pour the Champagne and cassis into a chilled champagne flute and stir briefly. Express the lemon zest over the drink and drop it into the glass.

— LIBATION NOTE —

Making a drink royal simply means that sparkling wine has been added to it. It works with any drink that could use a little lengthening or in which soda water is used.

STIRRUP CUP

SERVES **6**

At Downton, elegantly dressed ladies and gentlemen regularly romped through the countryside in pursuit of a fox before settling down to a hearty tea. Hunting tradition held that once the riders and hounds were all assembled at the meet, a drink would be handed round to send them on their way. Often it was just a simple drink of port. This cup, which comes from Henry Craddock's *The Savoy Cocktail Book* and was originally made with claret, veers dangerously into proper cocktail territory.

1¼ cups (10 fl oz/300 ml) ruby port

2½ fl oz (75 ml) maraschino liqueur

2½ fl oz (75 ml) curaçao

1½ barspoons superfine sugar

2½ cups (20 fl oz/600 ml) soda water, chilled

1 orange, thinly sliced in half wheels

6 pineapple rounds, peeled, and cut into eighths

½ cucumber, thinly sliced into wheels

Fresh mint sprigs, for garnish

Combine the port, maraschino liqueur, curaçao, and sugar in a punch bowl and stir until the sugar dissolves. Pour in the soda water and stir, then add ice and stir again. Add the orange, pineapple, and cucumber slices. Serve in cups, making sure to include some cucumber, orange, and pineapple in each cup. Garnish each cup with mint.

LIBATION NOTE

This drink is quite sweet,
so go easy on the
maraschino liqueur if you'd
prefer less sweetness.

COUPE

THE BOOTHBY

MAKES **1 COCKTAIL**

This variation on a Manhattan (page 147) strikes the right balance between sweet and bitter, and it lends a nice effervescence and sophistication worthy of a cocktail party. The recipe was developed by William "Cocktail Bill" Boothby, a bartender and author who tended bar at the Palace Hotel in San Francisco in the years just before the earthquake of 1906 reduced much of the city to ruins.

1½ fl oz (45 ml) rye whiskey or a high-rye Canadian whisky
1½ fl oz (45 ml) sweet vermouth

2 dashes Angostura bitters
1 fl oz (30 ml) sparkling wine (preferably brut), chilled

Combine the whiskey, vermouth, and bitters in a mixing glass filled with ice and stir until well chilled, 20–30 seconds. Strain into a chilled coupe or cocktail glass. Float the sparkling wine on top (see note, page 75).

— LIBATION NOTE —

To ensure the bubbles stay bubbly in the drink, make sure the sparkling wine and the cocktail are as cold as possible. Carbonation goes flat when the liquids are warm.

PINEAPPLE JULEP

SERVES **4**

Despite the "julep" in the name, this drink has nothing in common with other similarly named drinks, such as the Mint Julep on page 60, but is instead a punch. A recipe for it appears in William Terrington's 1869 *Cooling Cups and Dainty Drinks*, which was the earliest British book to include recipes for cocktails as well as other popular British and European libations.

1 pineapple, peeled and chopped

4 fl oz (120 ml) Bols barrel-aged genever

4 fl oz (120 ml) maraschino liqueur

4 fl oz (120 ml) raspberry syrup

Juice of 2 oranges

1 bottle (750 ml) sparkling wine, chilled

About 3⅓ cups (450 g) shaved or crushed ice

Seasonal berries, for garnish

Combine the pineapple, genever, maraschino liqueur, raspberry syrup, orange juice, wine, and ice in a punch bowl and stir to combine. Garnish with the berries. To serve, ladle into punch cups.

— LIBATION NOTE —

If you can't find barrel-aged genever, feel free to substitute your favorite whiskey here.

PLANTER'S PUNCH

MAKES **1 COCKTAIL**

This Jamaican drink seems to have inspired a legion to concoct the beverage. But oddly, there is no agreement on what the original recipe was, other than something vaguely tropical with citrus and rum. No two recipes are alike.

2 fl oz (60 ml) dark rum

2 fl oz (60 ml) fresh grapefruit juice

1 fl oz (30 ml) pineapple juice

1 fl oz (30 ml) fresh lime juice

½ fl oz (15 ml) simple syrup (see note, page 37)

1 fl oz (30 ml) club soda

Pineapple spear, for garnish

Combine the rum, fruit juices, and simple syrup in a shaker. Add ice, shake hard for 8–10 seconds, and strain into a collins glass filled with ice. Pour in the club soda and stir briefly. Garnish with the pineapple spear.

― LIBATION NOTE ―

Some recipes call for orange juice instead of grapefruit, lime juice instead of lemon, with grenadine as an additional sweetener. Feel free to experiment and find your own tropical escape.

FISH HOUSE PUNCH

SERVES **15–17**

This once-secret recipe was invented in 1732 at Philadelphia's venerable Fish House Club, which counted George Washington as a member. The drink packs a wallop, so make sure to sip slowly and to let the ice block dilute the punch.

2 bottles (750 ml each) dark rum

2¼ cups (525 ml) brandy

1 cup (240 ml) peach brandy

1¼ cups (300 ml) fresh lime juice

1¼ cups (300 ml) fresh lemon juice

1 cup (240 ml) simple syrup (see note, page 37)

¼ cup (60 ml) water

1 large ice block, for serving

Lemon and lime slices, for garnish

Pour the rum, both brandies, the citrus juices, the simple syrup, and the water into a large container made of stainless steel or other nonreactive material. Stir well, cover, and refrigerate until well chilled, at least 4 hours.

Place the ice block in the center of a large punch bowl, then pour in the punch and garnish with the citrus slices. Ladle into punch cups.

— LIBATION NOTE —

Peach brandy and peach liqueur are very different spirits, so be sure to get the unsweetened brandy, or cut the simple syrup amount in half if you can find only the liqueur.

PRINCE OF WALES PUNCH

SERVES **10**

Paying homage to the royal family was a tried-and-tested way to make a recipe sound suitably upmarket. The Prince of Wales is the title given to the (male) heir to the throne, who at the time of *Downton* was Edward, later Edward VIII, notable for his good looks, dapper dress sense, and many love affairs, often with married women. He appears briefly in *Downton* and is the reason for Lady Mary's brief career as a burglar, when she tries to retrieve one of his love letters, stolen from Freda Dudley Ward by the thoroughly villainous Terence Sampson during a party in London. This punch is light, refreshing, and ideal for those who don't like sweet cocktails. The very real Freda Dudley Ward was, like the fictional *Downton* daughters, born to an English father and American heiress mother. She was the prince's lover from 1918 until he fell in love with Wallis Simpson in 1934. Her husband divorced her on grounds of adultery in 1931.

1¾ cups (425 ml) Champagne

1¾ cups (425 ml) hock or other light Rhenish-style wine

2 fl oz (60 ml) brandy

2 fl oz (60 ml) curaçao

2 fl oz (60 ml) raspberry syrup

1 fl oz (30 ml) rum

Juice of ½ lemon

Juice of ½ orange

3½ cups (825 ml) soda water, chilled

Combine all the ingredients in a large container made of stainless steel or other nonreactive material, stir well, and serve in punch cups over ice.

COUPE

WHITE LADY

MAKES **1 COCKTAIL**

So famous was this drink at the American Bar at The Savoy in London that a cocktail shaker that held a White Lady was buried within the walls of the bar during a renovation in 1927.

2 fl oz (60 ml) gin
¾ fl oz (20 ml) fresh lemon juice

½ fl oz (15 ml) orange liqueur
1½ barspoons gum syrup (see note, page 36)

Combine all the ingredients in a shaker. Add ice, shake hard for 8–10 seconds, and strain into a chilled coupe or cocktail glass.

— LIBATION NOTE —

There are times when swapping out the simple syrup for liqueur sounds easier, but beware: Orange liqueurs are usually 80 proof, and increasing the amount to bump up the sweetness also adds alcohol. That minor addition can throw the drink off balance.

WEDDING COAT

MAKES **1 COCKTAIL**

Kindhearted, ethical, and efficient Mrs. Hughes always made sure the downstairs ran as smoothly as this cocktail. Based on the White Lady (page 103), the crème de cassis imbues the drink with floral and fruity notes that contrast nicely with the gin and gives it a lovely purple color.

2 fl oz (60 ml) gin
¾ fl oz (20 ml) fresh lemon juice

½ fl oz (15 ml) crème de cassis
1½ barspoons gum syrup (see note, page 36)

Combine all the ingredients in a shaker. Add ice, shake hard for 8–10 seconds, and strain into a chilled cocktail glass or coupe.

— LIBATION NOTE —

Much as with any piece of clothing, texture makes all the difference, and here the gum syrup turns this cocktail from a simple gin sour into a velvety classic, worthy of the finest celebration.

CARSON
But if I get my trousers wet?

MRS. HUGHES
If you get them wet, we'll dry them.

CARSON
Suppose I fall over?

MRS. HUGHES
Suppose a bomb goes off? Suppose we're hit by a falling star?
You can hold my hand. Then we'll both go in together.

CARSON
I think I will hold your hand. It'll make me feel a bit steadier.

— SEASON 4, EPISODE 9 —

4

THE
DRAWING ROOM

Predinner Drinks
& Hangover Helpers

MORNING GLORY FIZZ

MAKES **1 COCKTAIL**

This hangover remedy from the late nineteenth century is unique in its use of Scotch whisky, with the club soda designed both to settle the stomach and to provide lift to the drink. The nutmeg, preferably freshly grated, makes a big difference to the drink, so don't leave it out.

2 fl oz (60 ml) Scotch whisky

½ fl oz (15 ml) crème de cacao

1 fl oz (30 ml) light cream (see note, page 111)

4 fl oz (120 ml) club soda

Ground or freshly grated nutmeg, for garnish

Combine the whisky, crème de cacao, and cream in a shaker. Add ice, shake hard for 8–10 seconds, and strain into a collins glass or a double old fashioned glass over ice. Add the club soda and stir well. Sprinkle with the nutmeg.

LIBATION NOTE

This drink is very dry and refreshing, so if you would like it a touch sweeter, double the amount of crème de cacao.

BATES

Do you never doubt, for just one minute? I wouldn't blame you.

ANNA

No, and before you ask, I don't doubt that the sun will rise in the east, either.

— SEASON 3, EPISODE 1 —

NEVER DOUBT

MAKES **1 COCKTAIL**

There is no other relationship on *Downton Abbey* that withstands as many challenges as the one between Anna and John Bates. Despite Barrow's scheming, prison time for each of them, and the vindictive Vera, the pair manage to never doubt. This cocktail, which is based on the Morning Glory Fizz (page 108), honors that bond.

2 fl oz (60 ml) Cognac

1 fl oz (30 ml) orgeat syrup

1 fl oz (30 ml) light cream (see note)

4 fl oz (120 ml) club soda

Ground or freshly grated nutmeg, for garnish

Combine the Cognac, orgeat syrup, and cream in a shaker. Add ice, shake hard for 8–10 seconds, and strain into a collins glass over ice. Add the club soda and stir well. Sprinkle with the nutmeg.

— **LIBATION NOTE** —

Half-and-half or a mixture of equal parts whole milk and heavy cream works well if you cannot find light cream.

COUPE

CORPSE
REVIVER № 1

MAKES **1 COCKTAIL**

While there is nothing medicinal about this cocktail, despite its intended use to cure hangovers, there was plenty of medical drama when Downton Abbey housed a convalescence hospital for injured soldiers and Isobel Crawley helped out at the village hospital. This drink became popular when it was published in Harry Craddock's *The Savoy Cocktail Book* with this prescription: "To be taken before 11 a.m., or whenever steam and energy are needed."

1½ fl oz (45 ml) sweet vermouth	**¾ fl oz (20 ml) Calvados or other apple brandy**
	¾ fl oz (20 ml) Cognac

Combine all the ingredients in a mixing glass filled with ice and stir until well chilled, 20–30 seconds. Strain into a chilled coupe or cocktail glass.

LADY ANSTRUTHER
No cocktails? I thought everyone had them now.

MARY
Not at Downton. Our butler tried them once and he hasn't recovered.

— SEASON 5, EPISODE 1 —

COUPE

CLARKSON'S ANTIDOTE

MAKES **1 COCKTAIL**

Among classic cocktail enthusiasts, the Corpse Reviver No. 1 (see left) is considered a bit lackluster. By spotlighting the apple brandy with an entourage of supporting flavors—cinnamon from the bitters, vanilla from the dark rum, anise from the absinthe—this *Downton* variation, created in honor of Dr. Clarkson, is a lifesaver.

1½ fl oz (45 ml) sweet vermouth	**½ fl oz (15 ml) dark rum**
1 fl oz (30 ml) Calvados or other apple brandy	**¼ barspoon absinthe**
	2 dashes Angostura bitters

Combine all the ingredients in a mixing glass filled with ice and stir until well chilled, 20–30 seconds. Strain into a chilled coupe or cocktail glass.

ISOBEL
Will you really deny the man his chance of life?

CLARKSON
I just wish it was a treatment I was more familiar with.

ISOBEL
Will that serve as your excuse when he dies?

CLARKSON
Nurse! Will you prepare Mr. Drake for his procedure, please? Well, Mrs. Crawley, I have a feeling we will sink or swim together.

— SEASON 1, EPISODE 2 —

CORPSE REVIVER № 2

MAKES **1 COCKTAIL**

The drinks in this macabre series have nothing in common except that all of them are strong cocktails and meant to cure hangovers. New York–born Crosby Gaige, a bon vivant of the 1930s, once said that one Corpse Reviver would revive any self-respecting corpse, but that four taken in swift succession would return the corpse to a reclining position.

¾ fl oz (20 ml) gin
¾ fl oz (20 ml) Cocchi Americano
¾ fl oz (20 ml) orange liqueur

¾ fl oz (20 ml) fresh lemon juice
2 dashes absinthe

Combine all the ingredients in a shaker. Add ice, shake hard for 8–10 seconds, and strain into a chilled coupe or cocktail glass.

— LIBATION NOTE —

If you can't find Cocchi Americano or don't enjoy the quinine bitterness of the aperitif wine, you can substitute Lillet Blanc.

COUPE

PETRICK

MAKES **1 COCKTAIL**

The appearance of Major Peter Gordon, the mysterious Princess Patricia's Canadian Light Infantry burn victim at the Downton Abbey convalescent hospital, generates questions that never have a chance to be answered. Is he Patrick Crawley, who everyone believed died on the *Titanic*, back from the dead? Or is he Peter Gordon, who worked with Patrick at the Foreign Office? This cocktail, a twist on the Corpse Reviver No. 2 (page 114), doesn't take sides.

¾ fl oz (20 ml) Canadian whisky	¾ fl oz (20 ml) fresh lemon juice
¾ fl oz (20 ml) Cocchi Americano	2 dashes Angostura bitters
¾ fl oz (20 ml) orange liqueur	Ice cube, for garnish

Combine the whisky, Cocchi Americano, orange liqueur, lemon juice, and bitters in a shaker, add ice, and shake hard for 8–10 seconds. Strain into a chilled coupe or cocktail glass. Garnish with the ice cube (the "iceberg").

MARY

It's ridiculous. How can it be true? Where's he been hiding for the last six years?

EDITH

In Canada, suffering from amnesia.

ROBERT

He does have a story that would explain it, but I'm not quite sure about how to test the facts.

– SEASON 2, EPISODE 6 –

COLLINS

THE VALET

MAKES **1 COCKTAIL**

Like Mr. Bates, The Valet shares its heart with Anna's variation, the Never Doubt (page 111), which also calls for Cognac and orgeat syrup. This variation on the Ramos Gin Fizz (page 47) is bolder than the original because of the orgeat, which adds more texture than nutty flavor to the morning bracer.

2 fl oz (60 ml) Cognac
½ fl oz (15 ml) fresh orange juice
½ fl oz (15 ml) fresh lemon juice
½ fl oz (15 ml) orgeat syrup

4 drops orange flower water
1 egg white
**1 fl oz (30 ml) light cream
(see note, page 111)**
2 fl oz (60 ml) club soda

Combine the Cognac, citrus juices, orgeat syrup, orange flower water, egg white, and cream in a shaker. Add ice and shake hard for 3 minutes—or for as long as you can. Strain into a chilled collins glass. Add the club soda and stir briefly.

— **LIBATION NOTE** —

If you are concerned about the safety of using raw egg white here, or are simply planning on making lots of fizzes, buy a carton of pasteurized egg whites and use 1 fl oz (30 ml) for each drink.

GIN RICKEY

MAKES **1 COCKTAIL**

A member of the fizz family of mixed drinks, rickeys are made with a base spirit, fresh lime juice, and club soda and are garnished with a wedge of lime. This gin variation is the most popular drink in the fizz category, and it makes a very refreshing quaff while strolling the gardens on a hot summer day.

2 fl oz (60 ml) gin
1 fl oz (30 ml) fresh lime juice

5–6 fl oz (150–180 ml) club soda, chilled
Lime wedge, for garnish

Pour the gin and lime juice into an ice-filled collins glass. Add the club soda and stir briefly. Garnish with the lime wedge.

— LIBATION NOTE —

You'll notice this recipe uses no sweetener of any kind, making it a very dry drink that puts the focus on the spirit and little else. If it's too much, add some sweetener to make something more like the Raspberry Gin Fizz (see page 46).

BRANDY SHRUB

MAKES **3½ CUPS (825 ML)**

Not at all like a shrub in the modern sense (a sweet fruit vinegar to be mixed with soda water for a soft drink or with a spirit for a cocktail), this is nevertheless both fruity and fun. It is related to seventeenth- and eighteenth-century British shrubs, which were made of brandy or rum, citrus, and sugar, and it can be drunk neat by the hardcore, or used as a mixer with soda water, lemonade, or hot water to make a basic punch or cup. This version comes from Henry Craddock's *The Savoy Cocktail Book*, published in 1930.

1 pint (480 ml) brandy

Peel (in strips) and juice of 1 lemon

1 cup (240 ml) sherry

1 cup plus 2 tablespoons (225 g) sugar

Combine the brandy and lemon peel and juice in a tightly covered glass or ceramic container and let steep at room temperature for 3 days.

Strain the brandy mixture into a large jar, add the sherry and sugar, and cap tightly. Shake the jar a couple of times a day until the sugar is fully dissolved, up to 1 week. It's now ready to drink. Serve chilled in old fashioned glasses or in smaller pours in cordial or port glasses.

— LIBATION NOTE —

It's worth experimenting with mixers to work out which one suits you. Mixed with hot water, a slice of orange or lemon, and a slice of fresh ginger, this shrub also makes an excellent hot toddy for treating colds.

MOSELLE CUP

MAKES **2 COCKTAILS**

Cups were a popular mixed drink in Britain well before the advent of cocktails. They were drunk at parties and as an occasion drink, and they were also popular at picnics. Recipes tend to be vague—some wine, a spirit, and soda water over ice—so feel free to play with the amounts. This one uses Bénédictine, a French liqueur invented by a wine merchant in the late-Victorian period. He claimed it was based on a long-lost monastic manuscript, and he marketed it as a traditional health drink, with a secret recipe shrouded in mystery. It was made in Fécamp, in northern France, a town where many weary soldiers, war damaged and shell-shocked, were billeted after the armistice in 1918.

8 fl oz (240 ml) moselle or other sweet, light wine

8 fl oz (240 ml) soda water

2 fl oz (60 ml) Bénédictine

Fresh mint, borage, and/or lemon verbena sprigs and/or edible flowers, for garnish

Combine the wine, soda, and Bénédictine in a large mixing glass or a pitcher and stir well. Serve in collins glasses over ice. Decorate with the herb sprigs and/or flowers.

— LIBATION NOTE —

The garnish also flavors the drink, so it's important to use something you like (and that won't get in the way when you're drinking). Curls of orange or lemon zest or thin strips of cucumber will work as well.

UPSTAIRS COCKTAIL

COLLINS

MAKES **1 COCKTAIL**

There's no information on the Upstairs Cocktail in *The Savoy Cocktail Book*, recipe aside, but mixing up a couple of these reveals all you need to know: they are a refreshing and low-proof cocktail before dinner.

3 fl oz (90 ml) Dubonnet
½ fl oz (15 ml) fresh lemon juice

Seltzer water
Lemon twist, for garnish

Combine the Dubonnet and lemon juice in a collins glass with ice, then top off with the seltzer. Stir to mix. Express the lemon zest over the drink and drop it into the glass.

— LIBATION NOTE —

This drink would probably work fine with other fortified wine–based aperitifs or vermouths by simply adjusting the amount of seltzer you use.

ROBERT
Hello, Mama. Can I tempt you to one of these new cocktails?

VIOLET
No, no, I don't think so. They look too exciting for so early in the evening.

— SEASON 3, EPISODE 1 —

COLLINS

DONK

MAKES **1 COCKTAIL**

The two alcoholic beverages Lord Grantham loves the most are port and whisky, and this drink—fizzy and sweet with some nice acidity—manages to embrace both. It's a riff on the Upstairs Cocktail (page 122), with the whisky contributing heather, smoke, and turf, for contrast and depth.

½ fl oz (15 ml) fresh lemon juice

3 fl oz (90 ml) ruby port

Seltzer water

1½ barspoons peaty Scotch whisky

Lemon twist, for garnish

Combine the lemon juice and port in a collins glass with ice, then top off with the seltzer. Stir to mix. Float the whisky on top (see note, page 75). Express the zest over the drink and drop it into the glass.

— LIBATION NOTE —

The trivial amount of whisky may seem unnecessary, but it adds depth and aroma to the cocktail. Just don't stir the drink after adding the whisky.

OLD FASHIONED

KNICKERBOCKER

MAKES **1 COCKTAIL**

This refreshing cocktail from the late nineteenth century drinks like a proto-daiquiri (page 57), with just a hint of raspberry.

2 fl oz (60 ml) aged rum
½ fl oz (15 ml) fresh lime juice
1 barspoon raspberry syrup

1 barspoon curaçao
Seasonal berries, for garnish

Combine the rum, lime juice, raspberry syrup, and curaçao in a shaker. Add ice, shake hard for 8–10 seconds, and strain into an old fashioned glass. Garnish with the berries.

— **LIBATION NOTE** —

This makes for a very dry drink, so if you need something a little sweeter, add about ½ fl oz (15 ml) more raspberry syrup.

COUPE

BIJOU

MAKES **1 COCKTAIL**

First printed in the 1900 edition of Harry Johnson's *The New and Improved Illustrated Bartenders' Manual,* the Bijou is named for the French word for "jewel," which is perhaps overselling the drink's appearance. But this classic cocktail from the German-born American bartender is both simple and delicious. The book contains a comprehensive list of rules and regulations for running a bar, like the proper temperature to keep bitters, cordials, and syrups (room temp), plus recipes and advice in both English and German.

1 fl oz (30 ml) Plymouth gin	**Dash orange bitters**
1 fl oz (30 ml) green Chartreuse	**Cherry and lemon twist,**
1 fl oz (30 ml) sweet vermouth	**for garnish**

Combine the gin, Chartreuse, vermouth, and bitters in a mixing glass filled with ice and stir until well chilled, 20–30 seconds. Strain into a chilled coupe or cocktail glass. Garnish with the cherry, putting it directly into the glass, and then express the lemon zest over the drink and drop it into the glass.

— LIBATION NOTE —

Plymouth gin is both a brand and a style of gin made in the port city of Plymouth, in the southwest of England. A regional product that differs from standard London Dry gin, Plymouth gin is earthier, with less citrus, more roots, and lighter juniper flavor.

{Reggie's letter to Matthew}

I have few intimates, and so I've decided in her name, to add you to my list of heirs. I think it unlikely that I'll outlive both the first two, so there is little chance of your reading this letter, but if you do, and if the money has come to you, know it is with my full knowledge of what transpired.

Please do not allow any grief, guilt or regret to hold you back in its employment.

God bless you, my boy,

Reggie

— SEASON 3, EPISODE 3 —

COUPE

REGGIE'S LETTER

MAKES **1 COCKTAIL**

Poor, sweet Lavinia Swire gets caught in the middle of Mary and Matthew's destiny, much like how the sweet vermouth lands between the gin and the Chartreuse in the Bijou (page 127). Here, swapping it out for dry vermouth tones down the sweetness of the cocktail and gives it an herbal note that is both refreshing and elegant.

1 fl oz (30 ml) Plymouth gin
1 fl oz (30 ml) green Chartreuse
1 fl oz (30 ml) dry vermouth
Dash orange bitters

Cherry and lemon twist, for garnish
½ barspoon Fernet-Branca

Combine the gin, Chartreuse, vermouth, and bitters in a mixing glass filled with ice and stir until well chilled, 20–30 seconds. Strain into a chilled coupe or cocktail glass. Garnish with the cherry, putting it directly into the glass, and then express the lemon zest over the drink and drop it into the glass. Float the Fernet on top (see note, page 75).

— LIBATION NOTE —

If you carefully layer the Fernet on the surface of the cocktail, the amaro will float on top like a dark cloud, much like this letter (see left) to Matthew from Reggie Swire did. Thankfully, the cocktail doesn't taste like guilt or regret.

5

THE VILLAGE

Everyday Drinks

COLLINS

GINGER BEER

MAKES **7 PINTS (3.3 L)**

Ginger beer was a staple drink at fetes and fairs in the 1910s and 1920s. A favorite for the servants and the family alike, it was cheap to make, easy to keep, and refreshing to drink. We see it at nearly every village occasion on *Downton*, but also at more intimate settings, such as Harold Levinson's picnic with Madeleine Allsopp in season 4. This recipe was originally published in *The Field*, Britain's premier outdoor sports and country magazine.

3½ quarts (3.3 l) water

2½ tablespoons sugar

3 tablespoons ground ginger

Peel (coarsely grated or chopped) and juice of ½ lemon

1 teaspoon active dry yeast

1 small, thick slice yeast-risen white bread, toasted

Combine the water and sugar in a large saucepan and bring to a boil over high heat. Let cool to room temperature. Add the ginger and lemon peel and juice and stir to dissolve the ginger.

In a small bowl, stir together the yeast with just enough water to make a spreadable paste and spread the paste onto the toasted bread. Put the toast into the ginger mixture, then pour the ginger mixture into a bucket or large bowl and cover with a cloth. Leave at room temperature for 24 hours. Strain the mixture through a fine-mesh sieve. Rinse out the bucket or bowl, return the strained mixture to it, and re-cover it. Leave at room temperature for 4–5 days longer.

Strain it once again, this time more carefully, using a fine-mesh sieve lined with several sheets of paper towel. Pour into clip-top bottles, which will allow you to lessen the pressure if too much builds up. The beer is ready to drink immediately.

VIOLET

You are quite wonderful, the way you see room for improvement
wherever you look. I never knew such reforming zeal.

ISOBEL

I take that as a compliment.

VIOLET

I must have said it wrong.

— SEASON 1, EPISODE 5 —

IMPROVED GINGER BEER

MAKES **4 PINTS (2 L)**

A modern, easy take on ginger beer, this recipe requires minimal work and creates a flavorful drink—the perfect replacement for ginger ale. To spike a batch of ginger beer to serve bucks to your friends, add 2½ cups (600 ml) of your favorite spirit to the pitcher and stir well.

FOR THE GINGER SYRUP
**3 oz (90 g) fresh ginger
(about the size of a large finger)**
1 cup (200 g) sugar
½ cup (120 ml) water

2 pinches of salt
FOR THE GINGER BEER
6½ cups (1.5 l) club soda, chilled
½ cup (120 ml) fresh lime juice
Lime wheels, for garnish

To make the ginger syrup, put the ginger into a fine-mesh sieve set over a small jam or Mason jar. Using a small rubber spatula or your hand, press against the solids to extract as much liquid as possible. Cover and refrigerate the juice. Reserve the ginger solids.

Combine the sugar and water in a small saucepan over medium heat and bring to a boil, stirring to dissolve the sugar. Reduce the heat, stir in the salt and ginger solids, and simmer, stirring occasionally, for 5 minutes. Remove from the heat, cover, and let cool to room temperature.

Strain the syrup through the fine-mesh sieve set over the jar holding the ginger juice, pressing against the solids once again. Cover the jar tightly and shake well. You should have 1 cup (240 ml) syrup; it will keep refrigerated for up to 1 month. To make the ginger beer, combine the club soda, lime juice, and the ginger syrup in a pitcher and stir to mix well. Serve in a collins glass over ice, garnished with a lime wheel.

BLACK VELVET

MAKES **1 COCKTAIL**

This unlikely but elegant mixture of stout and sparkling wine was developed at Brooks's Club in London in 1861, to mourn the death of Prince Albert, Queen Victoria's prince consort. It is meant to symbolize the black band worn during mourning.

6 fl oz (180 ml) Irish stout, chilled

6 fl oz (180 ml) Champagne or sparkling wine, chilled

Carefully pour the stout and Champagne into a chilled pint glass or wineglass.

— **LIBATION NOTE** —

Sweeter sparkling wines work best here. If you're using dry sparkling wine, like a brut, add up to ½ fl oz (15 ml) simple syrup (see note, page 37) to the drink to help the flavors meld.

COUPE

ROB ROY

MAKES **1 COCKTAIL**

A twist on the Manhattan (page 147), the Rob Roy is said to have originated in 1894 at New York's Waldorf-Astoria hotel. Its inspiration was the Manhattan premiere of an operetta about the life of Rob Roy MacGregor, known as the Scottish Robin Hood.

2 fl oz (60 ml) blended Scotch whisky

1 fl oz (30 ml) sweet vermouth

2 dashes Angostura or other aromatic bitters

2 cherries, for garnish

Combine the whisky, vermouth, and bitters in a mixing glass filled with ice and stir until well chilled, 20–30 seconds. Strain into a chilled coupe or cocktail glass. Garnish with the cherries pieced together with a cocktail pick.

─ LIBATION NOTE ─

Try adding a float of peaty whisky on top (see note, page 75) for some additional complexity.

BLOODY MARY

MAKES **1 COCKTAIL**

Bartender Fernand Petiot reportedly created this classic in the 1920s at Harry's New York Bar in Paris, an American-style bar owned at the time by a former well-known American jockey, Tod Sloan. It has changed greatly over the years, and everyone seems to have a favorite take calling for an extra pinch of one seasoning or another. This recipe is basic but well balanced.

2 fl oz (60 ml) vodka

4 fl oz (120 ml) tomato juice

½ fl oz (15 ml) fresh lime juice

¼ barspoon black pepper

¼ barspoon ground cumin

Generous pinch of salt

2 dashes Worcestershire sauce

2 dashes hot sauce

Lime wedge, for garnish

Celery stalk, for garnish

Combine the vodka, tomato juice, lime juice, pepper, cumin, salt, Worcestershire sauce, and hot sauce in a shaker with ice and shake hard for 8–10 seconds. Pour the mixture, ice and all, into a pint glass. Garnish with the lime wedge and celery.

LIBATION NOTE

You can make up a batch of
Bloody Marys the night before
you plan to serve them, mixing
together everything but the lime
juice and garnishes and skipping
the ice. Refrigerate in a tightly
capped container. The next day,
add the lime juice and serve over
ice. Feel free to go crazy with the
garnishes, which can turn this
drink from hangover helper into
a full meal.

STOUT SANGAREE

MAKES **1 COCKTAIL**

Here is a hearty drink perfect for enjoying near the fireplace at the pub. It is part of the sangaree category of mixed drinks, whose members are all made with a base wine, spirit, or beer and a sweetening agent. In this version, ruby port adds sweetness and brightness to the mix. Sangarees (whose name is a variant of sangria) can be served over ice, neat, or straight up in a wineglass or beer glass.

1¼ cups (300 ml) Irish stout

3 fl oz (90 ml) ruby port

Ground or freshly grated nutmeg, for garnish

Pour the stout and port into a large wineglass. Sprinkle with the nutmeg.

— LIBATION NOTE —

If you suddenly find yourself living upstairs, replace the ruby port with tawny port, which is aged longer, so it oxidizes slightly and has a deeper, more complex flavor. But scale back the amount of stout to let the flavors of the port shine.

COLLINS

ORANGEADE

MAKES ¾ **CUP (180 ML)**

This orange syrup works great as a mixer, but it is just as good diluted with club soda as a refreshing nonalcoholic drink (see note). It calls for an old English technique in which sugar is used to extract the essential oils and flavor from citrus peel to create *oleo saccharum* (oil sugar).

1 orange

¼ cup (50 g) sugar

½ cup (120 ml) fresh orange juice, strained

¼ cup (60 ml) fresh lemon juice, strained

½ barspoon orange flower water

Using a vegetable peeler, remove the zest from the orange in wide strips and combine it with the sugar in a Mason jar. Using a wooden muddler or a wooden spoon, lightly mash together the zest and sugar. Cover the jar with a lid and let sit at room temperature for 24 hours, until the sugar is fully moistened and liquid has formed. Strain the mixture through a fine-mesh sieve, pressing against the solids to extract as much liquid as possible. Discard the zest.

Add the orange juice, lemon juice, and orange flower water to the zest-sugar liquid and stir to combine. It is best if the syrup is used right away, but it will keep in an airtight container in the refrigerator for up to 5 days.

--- **LIBATION NOTE** ---

To mix as a beverage, combine ¼ cup (60 ml) of the syrup with ¾ cup (180 ml) club soda in a collins glass filled with ice and stir briefly.

BOBBY BURNS

MAKES **1 COCKTAIL**

The Bobby Burns is a simple variation on the Rob Roy (page 137), dressed up with the addition of a little Bénédictine. The herbal liqueur became popular in England after World War I, particularly in the Burnley area, when injured soldiers from the East Lancashire Regiment developed a taste for it while recuperating at the Bénédictine distillery-turned-makeshift-hospital.

2 fl oz (60 ml) blended Scotch whisky

1 fl oz (30 ml) sweet vermouth

2 dashes Angostura or other aromatic bitters

1 barspoon Bénédictine, or ½ barspoon absinthe

2 cherries, for garnish

Combine the whisky, vermouth, bitters, and Bénédictine in a mixing glass filled with ice and stir until well chilled, 20–30 seconds. Strain into a chilled coupe or cocktail glass. Garnish with the cherries pieced together with a cocktail pick.

— **LIBATION NOTE** —

There are two versions of this drink, one from *The Savoy Cocktail Book* that calls for Bénédictine and one from the Waldorf-Astoria that uses ½ barspoon absinthe. The difference is slight but distinct. The absinthe makes the drink light and bright, while the Bénédictine version leans toward chocolate and dark fruit.

TOM AND JERRY

SERVES **24**

During the cold season, this early-nineteenth-century drink will warm you up. Although it is traditionally served from a Tom and Jerry bowl into Tom and Jerry cups, any bowl and mugs will work. Don't beat the egg whites here to stiff peaks. All you need to add to the batter is some volume. You don't need structure, like you would for a meringue.

12 eggs, separated
1½ cups (300 g) sugar
1 teaspoon baking soda
2 cups (480 ml) dark rum

2 cups (480 ml) brandy
2 quarts plus 1 cup (2.1 l) whole milk, scalded
Ground or freshly grated nutmeg, for garnish

In a large bowl, combine the egg yolks, 1¼ cups (250 g) of the sugar, and the baking soda and whisk until the mixture is thick and creamy.

In a Tom and Jerry bowl or other large bowl, using a handheld mixer on medium speed, beat the egg whites until frothy. Sprinkle in the remaining ¼ cup (50 g) sugar, raise the speed to medium-high, and beat until soft peaks form. Using a rubber spatula, fold the egg whites into the egg yolk mixture just until combined, forming a thick batter.

Whisking constantly, gradually add the rum and brandy to the batter.

Divide the batter evenly among 24 Tom and Jerry cups or heatproof punch cups (each should hold about ¾ cup/180 ml). Add about ⅓ cup (80 ml) hot milk to each cup (just pour it in, don't stir). Sprinkle the nutmeg over each serving.

OLD FASHIONED

MAKES **1 COCKTAIL**

If there were a First Earl and Countess of Grantham of cocktails, this would be it. The drink is an evolution of the sling, one of the earliest cocktails that simply combined spirits with water and sweetener. Adding bitters made it what today we know as an old fashioned. In the nineteenth century it was known as a bittered sling; calling it an old fashioned came later, when the drink was, by that time, old-fashioned.

1 sugar cube, ¾ barspoon granulated sugar, or 1 barspoon gum syrup

2 dashes bitters (usually Angostura)

1 large ice cube

2 fl oz (60 ml) whiskey

Lemon twist, for garnish

Put the sugar into an old fashioned or rocks glass, then add the bitters and a couple of dashes of water—just enough to moisten the sugar. Using a muddler, crush the sugar, dissolving it as much as possible. Add the ice cube and the whiskey and give everything a stir with a barspoon. Express the lemon zest over the drink and drop it into the glass.

— LIBATION NOTE —

This formula works with almost any unsweetened spirit and almost any sweetener, along with any bitters. It's the perfect prescription for experimenting to find what you like best.

MANHATTAN

MAKES **1 COCKTAIL**

The origins of the Manhattan are disputed, but the drink was developed sometime in the 1860s. It shows up in the 1887 edition of Jerry Thomas's *The Bar-Tenders Guide*, with the addition of a liqueur (Thomas suggests either curaçao or maraschino).

2 fl oz (60 ml) rye whiskey or a high-rye Canadian whisky

1 fl oz (30 ml) sweet vermouth

2 dashes Angostura bitters

2 cherries, for garnish

Combine the whiskey, vermouth, and bitters in a mixing glass filled with ice and stir until well chilled, 20–30 seconds. Strain into a chilled cocktail glass or coupe. Garnish with the cherries pieced together with a cocktail pick.

— LIBATION NOTE —

Originally made with rye whiskey, this recipe is the framework for other cocktails, including The Boothby (page 96), the Rob Roy (page 137), and the Bobby Burns (page 143).

DRY MARTINI

MAKES **1 COCKTAIL**

The classic and most famous of the cocktails, with a ratio of two parts gin to one part dry vermouth, is still one of the most elegant and sophisticated drinks around. While the gin is important, the vermouth is perhaps the most critical component. For silky martinis, keep your vermouth fresh and store it in the fridge.

2 fl oz (60 ml) gin
1 fl oz (30 ml) dry vermouth

Green cocktail olives or lemon twist, for garnish

Combine the gin and vermouth in a mixing glass filled with ice and stir until well chilled, 20–30 seconds. Strain into a chilled cocktail glass or coupe. Add the olives, pieced together with a cocktail pick if desired. If garnishing with a lemon twist, express the lemon zest over the drink and drop it into the glass.

— LIBATION NOTE —

If you enjoy your martinis with a lemon twist, try adding ½ fl oz (15 ml) blanc or bianco vermouth, which is sweeter, along with the dry vermouth.

TOM COLLINS

MAKES **1 COCKTAIL**

This drink is believed to be a variation on the John Collins (page 62), made with Old Tom gin instead of genever. That makes sense, given that genever is sweetened with malt wine and Old Tom is a sweetened gin. Here we stick with the modern interpretation, using London Dry gin and a hit of simple syrup.

2 fl oz (60 ml) London Dry gin

½ fl oz (15 ml) fresh lemon juice

½ fl oz (15 ml) simple syrup (see note, page 37)

5–6 fl oz (150–180 ml) club soda

Lemon wedge, for garnish

Combine the gin, lemon juice, and simple syrup in a shaker. Add ice, shake hard for 8–10 seconds, and strain into a collins glass filled with ice. Pour in the club soda and stir briefly. Garnish with the lemon wedge.

— **LIBATION NOTE** —

If you want to try it with Old Tom gin, just be aware that the Old Tom is sweeter than the standard London Dry varieties, so depending on the brand of gin, you may need to adjust the amount of simple syrup.

MUG

HOT BUTTERED RUM

MAKES **1 COCKTAIL**

This sweet, spice-laced, spiked beverage—also known as a hot toddy—has its origin in colonial America, where New England distillers were turning molasses imported from Jamaica into rum as early as the 1650s. The steaming-hot mix of the strong local spirit and rich butter provided a welcome defense against the bitter-cold Northeast winter. Don't be tempted to stir the melted butter into the drink. It should float on top.

2 fl oz (60 ml) dark rum

½ fl oz (15 ml) simple syrup (see note, page 37)

3 whole cloves

1 cinnamon stick, about 3 inches (7.5 cm) long

½–⅔ cup (120–160 ml) boiling water

1 barspoon (about 1 pat) unsalted butter (see note)

Ground or freshly grated nutmeg, for garnish

Pour the rum and simple syrup into a heatproof mug or an Irish coffee glass. Add the cloves and the cinnamon stick. Pour in the boiling water almost to fill the glass. Float the butter on top (so it will melt slowly), then sprinkle with the nutmeg.

— LIBATION NOTE —

Salted butter works well here, too, adding just enough salinity to brighten up the rum and spices.

APPLE HOT TODDY

MAKES **1 COCKTAIL**

Adapted from one of the oldest cocktail recipes, this version omits the mashing of the apple into the drink, drawing a majority of its apple flavor from the brandy instead. Feel free to mash the apple into the drink if you'd prefer. If you opt for tradition, keep the peel on, as it contains a good deal of the aroma and flavor of the fruit.

3 barspoons (½ oz/15 g) sugar

Boiling water, as needed

2 fl oz (60 ml) Calvados or other apple brandy

¼ baked apple

Whole nutmeg, for garnish

In a large heatproof mug, combine the sugar and a small amount of boiling water and stir until the sugar dissolves. Pour in the brandy and enough boiling water to fill the mug and stir well. Add the baked apple and grate a little nutmeg on top.

INDEX

ROSE

I love cocktail parties.

CORA

*Me, too. You only have to stay forty minutes, instead of
sitting for seven courses, between a deaf landowner and
an even deafer major general.*

— SEASON 5, EPISODE 5 —

weldon**owen**

President & Publisher **Roger Shaw**
Associate Publisher **Amy Marr**
Creative Director **Kelly Booth**
Art Director & Designer **Lisa Berman**
Photo Shoot Art Director **Marisa Kwek**
Managing Editor **Tarji Rodriguez**
Production Manager **Binh Au**
Production Designer **Carlos Esparza**

Drinks Photographer **John Kernick**
Food Stylist **Cyd Raftus McDowell**
Prop Stylist **Suzie Myers**

Produced by Weldon Owen
1150 Brickyard Cove Road
Richmond, CA 94801
www.weldonowen.com

Library of Congress Cataloging-in-Publication
data is available.
ISBN: 978-1-68188-998-6

Printed and bound in China
First printed in 2019
10 9 8 7 6 5 4

WRITTEN BY **LOU BUSTAMANTE**,
author of *The Complete Cocktail Manual*

WELDON OWEN WISHES TO THANK THE FOLLOWING PEOPLE FOR THEIR GENEROUS SUPPORT IN PRODUCING THIS BOOK

Julian Fellowes, Rizwan Alvi, Lisa Atwood, Debbie Berne, Lesley Bruynesteyn,
Annie Gray, Rishon Hanners, Rae Hellard, Rachel Markowitz, Joan Olson, Elizabeth Parson,
Nico Sherman, Sharon Silva, Josh Simons, Angela Williams, and Tammy White

CARNIVAL FILMS Gareth Neame, Aliboo Bradbury, Charlotte Fay, and Nion Hazell
NBCUNIVERSAL Dominic Burns
PETERS FRASER + DUNLOP Annabel Merullo and Laura McNeill
CUMBRIA CRYSTAL Chris Blade, Beverley Frankland, Carole Garnett, and Craig Hill
IMAGINE EXHIBITIONS Jay Hering, Jeffrey Millar, Whitney Sinkule, and Vince Quarta
HARROGATE TIPPLE Steven Green

THE OFFICIAL

DOWNTON ABBEY

AFTERNOON
TEA
COOKBOOK

FOREWORD BY GARETH NEAME

weldon**owen**

TABLE *of* CONTENTS

 1

2

3

4

MRS. PATMORE: *I've got tea for all of us,*
and a snack for you later on.

MASON: *You're an angel of mercy.*

~ SEASON 6, EPISODE 5

FOREWORD

Few customs are more iconic of England than the afternoon tea. Everything about it—the etiquette, the fine English china, the sandwiches and cakes—epitomizes some of the very best England has to offer.

Scenes of afternoon tea are prominently featured in *Downton Abbey*, all of them reflecting the height of fashion of the era. The word *'tea'* had long been used as an umbrella term for a variety of different occasions that involved tea drinking. It could be as modest as a cup of tea with a slice of cake at home or a pot of tea and some warm scones shared in a railway tearoom, or it could be a grand tea party held in the grounds of a great estate.

Downton Abbey gives the viewer a window into the tradition of this afternoon ritual both upstairs and downstairs. The servants' tea shows a rare moment of calm in the house, as the family upstairs can serve themselves as soon as the tea and food are displayed. Along with their cup of tea and a slice of bread or cake, the servants typically use the time to catch up on small tasks, such as mending a shirt and sewing on buttons. We see some footmen reading a newspaper, while others are lost in a book or sometimes playing cards.

For Violet, the Dowager Countess, afternoon tea visits are usually a moment for her to give grandmotherly advice or to meddle in family or village affairs. In season 3 episode 7, she summons Lady Edith to tea, during which she aims to convince her to look for a more suitable, lady-like occupation than becoming a columnist for *The Sketch*. Violet suggests running a charity or taking up watercolours. Edith listens, sips her tea, and then politely says she will take the job anyway.

Edith is breaking loose from the limitations that come with her social position as a woman from a great family. She symbolizes the modern times ahead in which women will not only gain more freedoms, but also the right to vote—a time when the corset and all it represents will finally be a thing of the past.

This little book is filled with recipes for many of the best offerings—biscuits and scones, cakes and tarts, savouries, preserves and more—that graced tea tables in the *Downton Abbey* era and continue to be enjoyed today. Just like the popular etiquette books of the time, these pages contain everything you need to know to organise your own proper afternoon tea.

GARETH NEAME
EXECUTIVE PRODUCER, *DOWNTON ABBEY* | LONDON, 2020

INTRODUCTION

When the Portuguese princess Catherine of Braganza arrived in England in 1662 to marry Charles II, she carried among her belongings a chest of tea. With it she would change English drinking habits forever—or so the legend goes and has been repeated for more than 350 years. The story of the Queen's tea chest became a marketing tool for the exotic beverage at court and among the upper classes. It even prompted politician and lyric poet Edmund Waller to write "Of Tea, Commended by Her Majesty" in 1663 to honor Catherine's contribution. But tea was already available in England, as it had been introduced to Europe in the seventeenth century through trade with China. The Portuguese court had embraced a tea culture early on, and the beverage soon spread to the rest of Europe.

A decade before Catherine's marriage, the first coffeehouse opened in London, and soon they were everywhere, though only men were permitted to enter them. Thomas Garway (sometimes spelled "Garraway"), who owned a coffeehouse in London's Exchange Alley, began selling tea leaves and offering tea as a drink in 1657, reportedly the first purveyor in England to do so. He put together a pamphlet that explained this new beverage to his customers, detailing its Chinese origin, medical virtues, and popularity with "Persons of quality," namely those who could afford the commodity and the precious imported chinaware to go with it. It would be nearly one hundred years before the first English-made porcelain teapots were manufactured that could stand up to the heat of boiling water without shattering. By then, tea drinking had become commonplace.

THE KEY TO FEMALE EMPOWERMENT

In a domestic environment, tea was considered a family drink and good for the health—a cure for colds and fevers and other maladies. The mistress of the house was responsible for managing its consumption, just as she was responsible for preparing other medicinal potions. This arrangement was in stark contrast to public tea consumption in the male-only coffeehouses and in the pleasure gardens of London, where both sexes engaged in the scandalous practice of tea drinking.

The mistress of the house kept the key to the tea caddy as a sign of control, and in paintings of the time, the caddy is always placed closest to the dominant female of the party, indicating her role as lady of the house. That control did not change until the nineteenth century, when the responsibility of overseeing the tea caddy was ceded to the housekeeper.

In the eighteenth century, it was common for fashionable ladies to get together at one another's homes for tea and conversation. Before that time, they had little or no social freedom and were often isolated. The safety of a nonalcoholic drink gave them the opportunity to gather and socialize.

The first known tea shop in London was opened in 1706 by Thomas Twining, and although it was a male-only environment, ladies came in their carriages to the back entrance, where their servants would discreetly buy the tea for them. The shop stood at 216 Strand, where it remains to this day.

The Twining family played an even greater role in Britain's becoming a tea-drinking nation when Richard Twining, grandson of Thomas and head of the tea trade, lobbied Prime Minister William

Pitt to reduce the tax on tea. He reportedly argued that revenues would be greater if taxes were lowered. Fraud and smuggling would no longer be profitable, which would put an end to sellers adding sloe leaves or the like to make the tea stretch further. As a result of the efforts of Twining and others, the Commutation Act of 1784 passed, which dropped the tax rate from 119 percent to 12.5 percent, making tea widely affordable and effectively ending smuggling and adulteration. The law's passage also increased the profits of the British East India Company, of which Twining was a director.

TEA MEETINGS

The nineteenth-century Temperance movement aggressively promoted tea as an alternative to beer, and large tea meetings were organized and managed by women. Originally used for fundraising, these get-togethers quickly became about power. In his 1884 *Tea and Tea Drinking*, Arthur Reade writes that there was "a spirit of rivalry among the ladies as to who should have the richest and most elegantly furnished table." He illustrates a few occasions when six hundred to twelve hundred people sat down for tea and for "singing hinnies [griddlecakes], hot wigs [small buns], and spice loaf, served up in tempting display."

TEA AT HOME

The Duchess of Bedford is often credited with having invented afternoon tea in 1842. She reportedly was the first to request something to eat—small cakes, delicate sandwiches—along with a pot of tea to battle a "sinking feeling" in midafternoon. But afternoon tea was actually the result of an evolution in British dining culture. Until the late eighteenth century, dinner was eaten at what we today call lunchtime, and it was followed by supper, which was a much later and lighter meal. Tea in accompaniment with bread and butter was already part of eighteenth-century visiting rituals, as dinner started to move further into the afternoon. By the end of the nineteenth century, dinner had migrated to the evening,

creating an opportunity for the well-to-do to dress up for the occasion.

The word *tea* could mean several things in the Victorian and Edwardian periods. Low tea, or what would later become known as afternoon tea, was so-called because the tea and the refreshments—cakes, buns, pastries, sandwiches—were served on low tables rather than at the dining table. *High tea*, a term now often mistakenly confused with afternoon tea, was a hearty meal of meat pies and other savory dishes, breads, and cheese eaten by the working classes at dinnertime.

Village afternoon teas were another well-established custom. These carefully orchestrated events were organized by women of the upper class for the poor, often to celebrate a major royal event, such as Queen Victoria's Golden Jubilee in 1887 and Diamond Jubilee in 1897. Such gatherings not only fulfilled these women's need to be engaged in some kind of charitable work but also provided a way for everyone—the haves and the have-nots—to show their patriotism to Crown and country. This tradition, minus the strict class structure, has continued into the twenty-first century, with large outdoor tea parties held in celebration of Queen Elizabeth's Golden, Silver, and Sapphire Jubilees.

The grandest of all teas was the afternoon tea party hosted on the grounds of a great estate. These elaborate gatherings were held for everything from a sporting event—such as Downton Abbey's annual cricket match—to a charity fundraiser to an engagement party. In season 1, episode 7, of *Downton Abbey*, at a garden party in aid of a local hospital, we see footmen circulating among the guests carrying silver trays with stacks of finger sandwiches, while visible on the table in the white marquee is a selection of Victoria sponges, ginger cakes, loaf cakes, and other sweets.

PUBLIC TEAROOMS

Tea meetings and village tea parties were both part of tea's moving outside the confines of the domestic household and into public spaces, such as railway refreshment rooms, hotel restaurants, and, by the 1860s, commercial tearooms. The Aerated Bread Company opened the first A.B.C. tea shop in a railway station in 1864, and by the *Downton Abbey* era, in the 1920s, its empire numbered some 250 tearooms. Although some establishments were grand enough to welcome Lady Mary and Matthew on a visit to London in season 3, episode 8, many of them emulated an upper-class environment on a smaller scale to attract the lower classes, creating the very British feeling of afternoon tea as a moment to dress up like the gentry.

Because the tearoom was a predominantly female environment, it became a natural meeting place for members of the suffragette movement—a place where they could come together without men to plan their "Votes for Women" fight. Women were on the move, as Lady Edith's story idea for her magazine illustrates in season 6, episode 5: "Victorian babies grown up into modern women."

THE CORSET AND THE TEA GOWN

Up until the early twentieth century, women typically wore corsets for most of their lives, which gave their bodies the hyperfeminine, perfectly contoured shape fashionable at the time. The garments were magnificent, but they were also shackles, placing the wearer in a state of imprisonment that made it difficult to walk, breathe, or look natural.

Despite the extreme discomfort, not all women were against the corset. Indeed, contemporary publications often presented both positive and negative views on its wearing. Societal norms leveled pressure too, with many people believing that corsets were a moral requirement, a symbol of decency, and to be seen without one in public would be vulgar.

While Lady Mary and Lady Edith don't mind strapping on a corset, we see Lady Sybil complaining about the tightness of hers in season

2. When she asks Anna to loosen it, Edith is quick to say, "It's the start of a slippery slope." This scene is symbolic of Sybil's personal struggle with the place of a woman in society—especially an upper-class woman. The suffragette movement is in the headlines, and the First World War will see women trade housework for factory work or train as nurses. Suddenly, a woman doesn't just have to be pretty or have to be the cook and maid. She can have a job, earn money, and be independent. For Sybil, training and working as a nurse gives her the liberation she has long sought. Even Edith loosens her corset when she changes into trousers and last season's coat and volunteers to drive a tractor to help John Drake, one of the estate's tenant farmers.

There were only two occasions on which a lady was not required to wear a corset. The first would be in her bedroom, when she wore a robe, one reason why married women like Cora and later Lady Mary liked to take their breakfast in bed, delaying donning a confining corset and a dress. The second would be for afternoon tea, when wearing a tea gown was the fashion.

The tea gown, which became popular in the mid-nineteenth century, borrowed its form from a variety of sources. Early examples were modeled on the Japanese kimono and were typically loose-fitting, flowing gowns of silk or chiffon. Later designs often mixed distinct aspects of different fashion periods, such as the eighteenth-century *robe à la française*, with its unfitted back and front, Watteau pleats, and frilly hanging sleeves. Waistlines could be empire style or dropped quite low, as was the rage in the 1920s. Although designed for afternoon tea, by the *Downton Abbey* era, tea gowns were also commonly worn throughout the afternoon and evening, and Cora is sometimes seen in a tea gown around the house.

TEA AT DOWNTON ABBEY

In *Downton Abbey*, we often get a glimpse of tea being served both upstairs and downstairs. In season 6, episode 4, Violet and Lady Shackleton are having tea, an occasion Violet is using to gain support that will allow her to manipulate a situation to her benefit. The silver hot-water kettle stands on a warmer, so the duo can serve themselves hot tea without the need for servants in the room. Meanwhile, downstairs, the servants are also having tea. Daisy is serving everyone, pouring tea from a tall Brown Betty teapot. While downstairs, the tea break is a rare moment of free time during a busy day, upstairs, the young women of the household find the afternoon tea a safe environment in which to socialize in a more natural manner, away from the strict protocol of dinner.

TEA ETIQUETTE

Books on social etiquette and the management of the household were popular in the days of *Downton Abbey*, but anyone born into a family like the Crawleys would have been raised to know these rules by heart at a young age. To need a book on etiquette was to mark you an outsider.

According to Emily Post's *Etiquette in Society, in Business, in Politics, and at Home*, published in 1922, the following items should always be present on the tea tray: "a kettle which ought to be already boiling, with a spirit lamp under it, an empty tea-pot, a caddy of tea, a tea strainer and slop bowl, cream pitcher and sugar bowl, and, on a glass dish, lemon in slices. A pile of cups and saucers and a stack of little tea plates, all to match, with a napkin . . . folded on each plate."

For the food, Post writes, there would be either a tea table or a stand made of three small "shelves," each large enough for one "good-sized plate." The top plate, covered, "holds hot bread of some sort; . . . the second dish usually holds sandwiches, and the third, cake. Or perhaps all the dishes hold cake; little fancy cakes for instance, and pastries and slices of layer cakes." At Downton, we often see trays of small cakes, Victoria sponge, or fruitcake.

PREPARING THE TEA

- Bring a kettle filled with fresh cold water to a boil. If desired, pour a little boiling water into your teapot, swirl it around to warm the pot, and then pour it out.

- Add to the warmed teapot 1 teaspoon tea leaves per person plus 1 teaspoon for the pot.

- As soon as the water returns to a boil, pour it over the leaves in the pot.

- Allow the tea to steep for 2–5 minutes, depending on the preferred strength and the type of tea (black teas are typically steeped longer than white, green, or oolong teas). Set a pitcher filled with hot water on the tea tray so that guests who favor a weaker cup can dilute their serving.

SERVING THE TEA

The hostess traditionally both makes and pours the tea, a holdover from the days when women held the key to the tea caddy and therefore the power of the house. Each cup is poured—ideally through a tea strainer to capture loose leaves—and passed to a guest before the next cup is poured.

A guest then adds milk or a lemon slice to the cup. Milk is typically added to black tea, while lemon is traditionally paired with Lapsang Souchong. (In the past, before heat-resistant porcelain was commonplace, milk was added to the cup before the hot tea to guard against the china breaking.) Sugar is added last, and the tea is then stirred. Once the sugar has dissolved, the spoon is returned to the saucer.

The saucer always remains on the table when the cup is lifted to drink. The cup is grasped with the thumb and index finger meeting in the handle and the handle resting on the middle finger. Contrary to popular belief, the pinkie should never be held upright, which is considered rude. Finally, tea is sipped, not gulped, and the cup is returned to the saucer between sips.

BRITISH TEA CHARACTERISTICS

The first tea to arrive in England from China was green tea in the seventeenth century. The strong black tea that is now associated with English tea drinking is a legacy of British tea production in colonial India in the nineteenth century.

By the early nineteenth century, the British had developed such a taste for tea that they knew they had to expand their source beyond China. In the 1820s, the British East India Company, already established in colonial India, began extensive production in Assam using a local tea variety. The new enterprise flourished, delivering not only a steady supply of tea at a lower price to the home market but also a patriotic product for the empire.

In the late 1840s, the British East India Company, recognizing China's commanding expertise in the production and processing of tea, sent the Scottish botanist Robert Fortune to China to learn all he could about Chinese tea horticulture and manufacturing and to obtain the finest plants for replanting in India. Although Fortune arranged for thousands of tea plants to be shipped to India, all but a handful died. But the knowledge he had acquired and the experienced Chinese workers he brought to Assam to oversee processing paved the way not only for India to become one of the world's premier tea producers but also for tea to become part of everyday life across the British classes.

TYPES OF TEA

While traditional caffeinated teas are made from just two varieties of the *Camellia sinensis* tea plant, *C. sinensis* var. *sinensis* (Chinese tea) and *C. sinensis* var. *assamica* (Indian Assam tea), they yield a variety of different types of tea as a result of how the leaves are processed and blended.

GREEN TEA

Green tea originated in China and then spread to many other countries in Asia. It calls for very little processing apart from drying or steaming the leaves and then rolling them.

WHITE TEA

Once known as silvery tip pekoe because of its appearance, white tea is the lightest flavored of the five primary types. It is made from immature leaves and young buds covered with fine white hairs, both harvested by hand before they fully open and then minimally processed by quickly being dried.

BLACK TEA

Generally stronger in flavor than the other types, black tea undergoes four stages in processing: first the leaves are heavily withered, next they are tightly rolled, then they are allowed to oxidize completely under controlled temperature, and finally they are dried to stop the oxidation process.

OOLONG TEA

These leaves are allowed to oxidize partially and ferment under controlled temperature, after which they are curled and twisted to create their unique shape.

LAPSANG SOUCHONG

For this black tea, the rougher leaves of the tea plant are withered, rolled, oxidized, and then roasted over a pinewood fire, resulting in a distinctive smoky flavor.

BLENDED TEA

EARL GREY

Prized for its citrus notes, which it owes to the addition of bergamot (natural or synthetic), Earl Grey, the first mention of which appeared in the 1880s, was originally made from Keemun, a Chinese tea. To make it more appealing with milk, tea companies switched to a more boldly flavored black tea, which nowadays might be Ceylon, African, or Indian tea.

ENGLISH BREAKFAST

Despite the name, English breakfast tea, which dates to the late eighteenth century, first appeared in America, not Britain. It is a full-flavored tea made from Assam, Ceylon, and Kenya black teas, sometimes with the addition of milder Keemun.

IRISH BREAKFAST

A blended black tea made mostly from Assam, Irish breakfast is characterized by its red color and robust malty flavor that are perfect with the addition of milk.

PASTRIES, BUNS
& BISCUITS

ENGLISH CREAM SCONES

Scones have been essential to the British teatime tradition since the mid-nineteenth century, when, according to legend, the fashionable Duchess of Bedford ordered her servants to sneak the small cakes and hot tea into her room for an afternoon snack. In time, she began inviting her friends to join her for afternoon tea, and this homey ritual became a social trend. Queen Victoria, hearing of the new convention, soon began hosting fancy-dress tea parties. The tradition continued into the twentieth century, with Mrs. Patmore serving scones to Lord and Lady Grantham at her bed-and-breakfast in season 6 of *Downton Abbey*.

2 cups (250 g) flour, plus more for the work surface

1 tablespoon baking powder

2 teaspoons sugar, plus 1 tablespoon for sprinkling

1 teaspoon salt

½ cup (70 g) dried currants

¾ cup plus 2 tablespoons (200 ml) heavy cream

FOR THE TOPPING

1 egg white, lightly beaten with 1 teaspoon water

MAKES 10 SCONES

TEA ETIQUETTE

A scone should always be torn in two rather than cut with a knife, which would make the scone seem heavy.

Preheat the oven to 425°F (220°C). Have ready an ungreased sheet pan.

In a large bowl, whisk together the flour, baking powder, the 2 teaspoons sugar, and salt. Using a large spoon, stir in the currants and cream just until combined. Using your hands, gently gather the dough together, kneading it against the side of the bowl until it holds together in a rough ball.

Lightly flour a work surface and turn the dough out onto it. Roll out the dough about ¾ inch (2 cm) thick. Using a 3-inch (7.5-cm) round cutter, cut out rounds from the dough, pressing straight down and lifting straight up and spacing them as closely together as possible. Place the dough rounds at least 2 inches (5 cm) apart on the sheet pan. Gather up the dough scraps, knead briefly on the floured work surface, roll out the dough again, cut out more rounds, and add them to the pan.

Using a pastry brush, lightly brush the tops of the scones with the egg white mixture, then sprinkle evenly with the remaining sugar.

Bake the scones until golden, 10–12 minutes. Transfer to a wire rack to cool. Serve warm or at room temperature.

MADELEINES

These seashell-shaped French tea cakes were a customary addition to the afternoon tea tray at Downton and were kept in biscuit jars by the beds of Mary, Edith, and Sybil for late-night snacking. They were also a favorite of Matthew whose middle-class upbringing showed when, on his first visit to Downton, he loaded up his plate with the small, delicate cakelike madeleines.

4 tablespoons (60 g) unsalted butter, melted and cooled, plus room-temperature butter for the pan

½ cup (60 g) flour, plus more for the pan

2 eggs

⅓ cup (70 g) granulated sugar

¼ teaspoon salt

1 teaspoon pure vanilla extract

Confectioners' sugar, for dusting (optional)

MAKES 12 MADELEINES

Preheat the oven to 375°F (190°C). Using a pastry brush, coat the 12 molds of a madeleine pan with room-temperature butter, carefully coating each and every ridge. Dust the molds with flour, tilting the pan to coat evenly and then tapping out the excess.

In a bowl, using an electric mixer, beat together the eggs, granulated sugar, and salt on medium-high speed until light and fluffy, about 5 minutes. Beat in the vanilla. Turn off the mixer and sift the flour over the egg mixture. With the mixer on low speed, beat in the flour until fully incorporated. Turn off the mixer again and, using a rubber spatula, gently fold in half of the melted butter just until incorporated. Fold in the remaining melted butter just until blended.

Scoop a heaping tablespoonful of the batter into each prepared mold. Bake the madeleines, rotating the pan back to front halfway through baking, until the tops spring back when lightly pressed with a fingertip, 10–12 minutes. Remove the pan from the oven, immediately invert it onto a wire rack, and tap the pan on the rack to release the madeleines. If any of them stick, turn the pan upright, loosen their edges with a butter knife, and then invert and tap again. Let cool completely. If desired, lightly dust the tops with confectioners' sugar just before serving.

ENGLISH TOFFEE SHORTBREAD

The Scottish shortbread favored by Mary, Queen of Scots (see page 36), saw only minor changes until the twentieth century. One nineteenth-century variation that included ginger was favored by members of the Scottish Parliament, earning the snack the name Parliament Cakes. For this later innovation, a much-celebrated English candy, which even boasts its own holiday, National English Toffee Day, is mixed into the dough.

½ cup (115 g) cold unsalted butter, cut into cubes, plus room-temperature butter for the pan

1 cup (125 g) flour, plus more for pressing

⅓ cup (80 g) firmly packed light brown sugar

2½ tablespoons cornstarch

⅛ teaspoon kosher salt

¾ teaspoon pure vanilla extract

½ cup (60 g) coarsely chopped pecans

⅓ cup (60 g) finely chopped chocolate-covered English toffee

Granulated sugar, for sprinkling

MAKES 16 BARS

Preheat the oven to 350°F (180°C). Butter a 9-inch (23-cm) square or round cake pan.

In a food processor, combine the flour, brown sugar, cornstarch, and salt and process until blended, about 5 seconds. Scatter the cold butter over the flour mixture, add the vanilla, and, using rapid pulses, process until the mixture resembles fine meal. Add the pecans and process until finely chopped. Add the toffee and process just to incorporate.

Using lightly floured fingertips, press the dough into the prepared pan in an even layer. Sprinkle the surface evenly with granulated sugar.

Bake the shortbread just until it begins to color and the edges are golden, about 20 minutes. Let cool in the pan on a wire rack for 5 minutes, then cut into 16 bars or wedges, carefully transfer the bars to the rack, and let cool completely.

ROCK CAKES

The origin of these small, fun, craggy cakes is unknown, though they seem to date from at least the mid-eighteenth century. The dough comes together quickly with the help of a food processor, but it can also be made by hand, using your fingers to rub the flour mixture and butter together. Any type of dried fruit or combination of dried fruits can be used. Currants, golden raisins, cherries, apricots, and cranberries are good choices.

1¾ cups (220 g) flour, plus more for rolling

¼ cup (50 g) granulated sugar

1¾ teaspoons baking powder

¼ teaspoon salt

½ cup (115 g) cold unsalted butter, diced

½ cup (70 g) dried fruit of choice, in small pieces

1 egg, lightly whisked

2 tablespoons milk

Sanding sugar, for sprinkling (optional)

MAKES 12 SMALL CAKES

Preheat the oven to 375°F (190°C). Line two sheet pans with parchment paper or silicone mats.

In a food processor, combine the flour, granulated sugar, baking powder, and salt and process until blended, about 5 seconds. Scatter the butter over the flour mixture and process until the mixture resembles coarse meal, 8–10 seconds. Dump the mixture into a bowl and stir in the dried fruit. Pour the egg and milk over the top and, using a rubber spatula and one hand, mix and pinch until all the ingredients come together in a soft dough.

Divide the dough into 12 equal pieces (about 3 tablespoons each) and gently shape each piece into a mound. Arrange the mounds on the prepared pans, spacing them about 2½ inches (6 cm) apart. Sprinkle with the sanding sugar, if using.

Bake the cakes until golden brown and a toothpick inserted into the center of a cake comes out clean, 16–18 minutes. Let cool on the pans on wire racks for at least 5 minutes. Serve warm or at room temperature.

RECIPE NOTE

If you have not sprinkled the cakes with sanding sugar, they can be served warm from the oven lightly dusted with confectioners' sugar. They can also be smeared with butter and a smidgen of jam. They are best served the day they are baked and can be reheated in a low oven.

WELSH CAKES

The texture of these Welsh griddle cakes lies between that of a pancake and that of a biscuit or scone. This version is slightly sweeter than the traditional one and is delicious for both breakfast and teatime, especially on March 1, the feast day of Saint David, the patron saint of Wales. Serve them straight from the griddle as they are or sprinkled with confectioners' or cinnamon sugar.

1½ cups (190 g) flour, plus more for the work surface

¼ cup (50 g) sugar

1¼ teaspoons baking powder

¼ teaspoon salt

Pinch of ground nutmeg (optional)

½ cup (115 g) cold unsalted butter, diced, plus more for cooking

⅓ cup (45 g) dried currants

1 egg, lightly whisked

¼ cup (60 ml) milk

MAKES TEN 2¼-INCH (5.5-CM) CAKES

In a food processor, combine the flour, sugar, baking powder, salt, and nutmeg (if using) and process until blended, about 5 seconds. Scatter the butter over the flour mixture and process until the mixture resembles coarse meal, 8–10 seconds. Transfer the mixture into a bowl and stir in the currants. Pour the egg and milk over the top and, using a rubber spatula and one hand, mix and pinch until all the ingredients come together in a soft, slightly sticky dough.

Scrape the dough onto a lightly floured work surface and press into a round about ½ inch (12 mm) thick, lightly flouring as necessary. Using a 2¼-inch (5.5-cm) round cutter, cut out as many rounds as possible. Gather together the scraps, press together into a round about ½ inch (12 mm) thick, and cut out more rounds. You should have a total of 10 rounds.

Heat a griddle or a cast-iron frying pan over medium-low heat. Drop a small piece of butter onto the hot surface and spread to coat the surface. Add as many cakes as will fit without crowding and cook until deep golden brown on the bottom, about 4 minutes. Reduce the heat if overbrowning. Flip the cakes and continue cooking until they are puffed, the underside is golden brown, and the sides no longer look wet, 4–5 minutes longer, adjusting the heat if necessary.

Transfer the cakes to a wire rack and let cool for 5 minutes before serving. Repeat with the remaining cakes, adding more butter to the griddle as needed. Serve warm.

PALMIERS

In Edwardian England, the ability to produce refined French pastry, such as the puff pastry used for *palmiers,* was an essential skill of cooks in the houses of the aristocracy. Although *palmier* is French for "palm tree," these flaky, crunchy cookies have taken on many names across the world, from pig's ears, elephant's ears, and *coeurs de France* to shoe soles, eyeglasses, and more.

2 tablespoons unsalted butter, melted

½ teaspoon pure vanilla extract

½ cup (100 g) granulated sugar

½ cup (60 g) confectioners' sugar

1 sheet frozen puff pastry, about ½ lb (225 g), thawed

1 egg, beaten with 1 tablespoon water

MAKES ABOUT 20 PALMIERS

TEA ETIQUETTE

The Crawleys use both their more elegant silver tea set as well as porcelain cups, saucers, and plates.

Preheat the oven to 375°F (190°C). Line two sheet pans with parchment paper.

In a small bowl, stir together the butter and vanilla. In another bowl, using a fork, stir together the granulated and confectioners' sugars. Measure out ½ cup (80 g) of the sugar mixture and set aside.

Sprinkle 3 tablespoons of the remaining sugar mixture onto a work surface. Place the puff pastry on top of the sugared surface. Sprinkle more of the sugar mixture on top of the pastry, spreading it evenly with your hands. Using a rolling pin and starting at the center of the pastry sheet, roll out the pastry into a 10-by-20-inch (25 x 50-cm) rectangle, always rolling from the center outward and rotating the sheet a quarter turn after every one or two passes with the pin. As you work, sprinkle a little more sugar mixture underneath and on top of the pastry as needed to prevent sticking.

Using a pastry brush, brush the butter mixture over the surface of the pastry. Sprinkle evenly with the reserved ½ cup (80 g) sugar mixture. Starting at one short end, fold a band of the pastry 2 inches (5 cm) wide over onto itself. Repeat this folding until you reach the center of the pastry. Fold the other end of the rectangle in the same way. Turn the folded side down and cut the rectangle crosswise into slices ½ inch (12 mm) thick. Place the slices on the prepared pans, spacing them 2 inches (5 cm) apart.

Bake the palmiers until golden, about 15 minutes. Let cool on the pans on wire racks for 5 minutes, then transfer them to the racks and let cool completely.

HOT CROSS BUNS

These sweet spiced buns, a hallmark of the Easter season, became popular in England in the seventeenth century, when rich yeast-risen doughs were in vogue. Perhaps even more commonly enjoyed for breakfast than for afternoon tea, hot cross buns were a staple of the Downton tables, both upstairs and downstairs, and were regularly seen cooling in Mrs. Patmore's kitchen.

3½–4 cups (440–500 g) flour, plus more for the work surface and bowl

¼ cup (50 g) superfine sugar

½ teaspoon ground nutmeg

½ teaspoon ground cinnamon

¼ teaspoon ground ginger

Generous pinch of salt

4 tablespoons (60 g) salted butter, plus more for the pan and for serving

1¼ cups (300 ml) milk

1 teaspoon active dry yeast

1 egg, lightly whisked

½ teaspoon grated lemon zest

½ teaspoon grated orange zest

½ cup (80 g) firmly packed dried currants

½ cup (90 g) diced mixed candied orange and lemon peel or golden raisins

MAKES 12 BUNS

In a large bowl, stir together 3½ cups (440 g) of the flour, the sugar, nutmeg, cinnamon, ginger, and salt, mixing well. Make a well in the center.

In a small saucepan over medium heat, combine the butter and milk and heat just until the butter melts. Remove from the heat and let cool to barely lukewarm (100°F/38°C), then add the yeast. Let stand until the yeast is foamy, about 5 minutes, then add the egg and citrus zests and stir until well mixed. Pour the yeast mixture into the well in the flour mixture and stir together with a wooden spoon until a shaggy dough forms.

Flour a work surface, turn the dough out onto it, and knead until smooth, soft, and elastic, about 20 minutes, adding only as much of the remaining ½ cup (60 g) flour, a little at a time, as needed to prevent sticking. Lightly flour a large bowl and transfer the dough to it. Cover the bowl with plastic wrap or a damp kitchen towel, set the bowl in a warm spot, and let the dough rise until doubled in size, about 1½ hours.

Lightly flour the work surface, turn the dough out onto it, and press the dough flat. Scatter the currants and candied peel evenly on top. Roll up the dough to enclose the fruits, then knead gently to distribute the fruits evenly. Cover with a bowl or a damp kitchen towel and let rest for 10 minutes.

Lightly butter a sheet pan. Divide the dough into 12 equal portions and shape each portion into a ball. As the balls are formed, place them, seam side down, on the prepared pan, spacing them evenly apart. Cover them loosely with a damp kitchen towel and leave them to rise in a warm spot until puffy, about 1 hour. After about 40 minutes of rising, preheat the oven to 375°F (190°C).

Using a very sharp knife, slash a cross in the top of each raised bun. Bake the buns until golden brown, 15–20 minutes. Transfer to a wire rack, let cool slightly, and eat hot, or let cool completely on the rack and serve at room temperature. Either way, offer butter at the table for slathering onto the buns.

GINGER BISCUITS

Also known as ginger nuts, these hard spiced biscuits (aka cookies) have been popular in Britain since the 1840s. Although similarly spiced, they are quite different from gingerbread, which is thicker and has a softer, breadlike texture. These no-frill sweets emerge from the oven quite soft but harden on cooling, making them perfect for dunking into a hot cup of afternoon tea.

2½ cups (310 g) flour

1½ teaspoons ground ginger

1 teaspoon baking soda

½ teaspoon ground cinnamon

¼ teaspoon ground cloves

¼ teaspoon salt

⅔ cup (160 ml) canola oil

1 cup (210 g) firmly packed light brown sugar

⅓ cup (115 g) dark molasses (black treacle)

1 whole egg, lightly whisked

¾ cup (130 g) chopped crystallized ginger

1 egg white

½ cup (115 g) coarse sugar

MAKES ABOUT 48 BISCUITS

Preheat the oven to 325°F (165°C). Line two sheet pans with parchment paper.

Combine the flour, ground ginger, baking soda, cinnamon, cloves, and salt in a sifter or fine-mesh sieve and set aside.

In a large bowl, using a wooden spoon, stir together the oil, brown sugar, and molasses until well combined. Add the whole egg and beat until blended. Sift the flour mixture into the oil mixture and stir until blended. Stir in the crystallized ginger.

In a small bowl, lightly whisk the egg white. Spread the coarse sugar in a shallow bowl.

With dampened hands, shape the dough into 1-inch (2.5-cm) balls. Brush each ball lightly with the egg white and then roll in the sugar to coat lightly. Place the dough balls about 1 inch (2.5 cm) apart on the prepared pans.

Bake the biscuits until the tops are set and crackled, 15–18 minutes. Let cool on the pans on wire racks for 5 minutes, then transfer to the racks and let cool completely, until firm.

CHOCOLATE FLORENTINES

Despite the seemingly eponymous name, not much is known about these elegant treats except that Florentines do not hail from Florence. Although their origin is a mystery, the thin, crisp, and delicate nature of the caramelized almond delicacies suggests both French pastry technique and a place on the afternoon tea menu.

FOR THE FLORENTINES
1 teaspoon grated orange zest

¼ cup (30 g) flour

5 tablespoons (70 g) unsalted butter, cut into pieces

¼ cup (60 ml) heavy cream

½ cup (100 g) sugar

2 tablespoons honey

¾ cup (70 g) sliced blanched almonds

FOR THE CHOCOLATE GLAZE

6 oz (170 g) semisweet chocolate, finely chopped

½ cup (115 g) unsalted butter

1 tablespoon light corn syrup

MAKES ABOUT
24 FLORENTINES

Preheat the oven to 325°F (165°C). Line two sheet pans with parchment paper.

To make the Florentines, in a small bowl, stir together the orange zest and flour until the zest is coated. Set aside.

In a saucepan over low heat, combine the butter, cream, sugar, and honey. Cook, stirring, until the butter melts and the sugar dissolves. Raise the heat to medium-high and bring to a boil, stirring constantly, then boil for 2 minutes. Remove from the heat and stir in the almonds, followed by the flour mixture. The batter will be thick. Drop the batter by 2-teaspoon scoops onto the prepared pans, spacing the Florentines about 3 inches (7.5 cm) apart. Flatten each Florentine with the back of the spoon.

Place one sheet pan in the oven and bake the cookies until they spread to about 3 inches (7.5 cm) in diameter, are bubbling vigorously, and are light brown at the edges, about 14 minutes. Let the Florentines cool on the pan on a wire rack for 10 minutes. Using a wide spatula, transfer them to the rack and let cool completely. Repeat with the second sheet pan.

To make the glaze, combine the chocolate, butter, and corn syrup in a heatproof bowl placed over (not touching) barely simmering water in a saucepan and heat, stirring often, until the chocolate and butter are melted, about 4 minutes. Remove from the heat and pour the glaze through a fine-mesh sieve into a heatproof bowl. Let cool to barely lukewarm before using.

Line a sheet pan with parchment paper. Dip half of each Florentine into the lukewarm glaze and place on the prepared pan. Let stand until the glaze sets, about 30 minutes.

SCOTTISH SHORTBREAD

Shortbread dates back to a hard, dry, sugar-dusted twelfth-century Scottish yeasted biscuit. In the mid-sixteenth century, Mary, Queen of Scots, encouraged her French pastry chefs to create a more refined version in which the yeast was traded out for butter and the dough was baked into a round, scallop-edged cake that was cut into wedges for serving. The last major change came in 1921, when British law mandated that any product labeled "shortbread" must derive at least 51 percent of its fat from butter, guaranteeing Downton residents a properly buttery treat.

1½ cups (190 g) flour, plus more for pressing

¼ teaspoon salt

1 cup (225 g) unsalted butter, at room temperature

¼ cup (30 g) confectioners' sugar

¼ cup (50 g) granulated sugar, plus 1 tablespoon for sprinkling

2 teaspoons pure vanilla extract

MAKES 12–16 BARS

Preheat the oven to 300°F (150°C). Have ready a 9-inch (23-cm) square baking pan.

Sift together the flour and salt into a bowl. In a large bowl, using an electric mixer, beat the butter on medium-high speed until fluffy and pale yellow, about 3 minutes. Add the confectioners' sugar and the ¼ cup (50 g) granulated sugar and beat until the mixture is well combined, then beat in the vanilla. On low speed, gradually add the flour mixture and beat just until blended.

Using lightly floured fingertips, press the dough into the baking pan in an even layer. Sprinkle the surface evenly with the remaining 1 tablespoon granulated sugar.

Bake the shortbread until the edges are golden, about 1 hour. Remove from the oven and, using a thin-bladed, sharp knife, immediately cut the shortbread into 12–16 bars. Using a fork, decorate each bar with a pattern of dots. Let cool in the pan on a wire rack for 30 minutes, then carefully transfer the bars to the rack and let cool completely.

PECAN TUILES

Tuiles, French for "tiles," are wafer-thin cookies arced to mimic the roof tiles on French country homes. The well-traveled members of the Crawley household would likely have been just as familiar with the delicate rounded sweets served in the best patisseries as they were with French architectural style. Pecans made their way to Europe from North America in the sixteenth century with returning Spanish explorers. Although tuiles are traditionally made with almonds, an innovative Parisian pastry chef would have hit upon the idea of using the New World nut in their place.

½ cup (60 g) pecans, plus ⅓ cup (40 g) finely chopped

½ cup (100 g) sugar

¼ cup (30 g) flour

5 tablespoons (70 g) unsalted butter, melted and cooled, plus room-temperature butter for the pan

2 egg whites, lightly whisked

½ teaspoon pure vanilla extract

MAKES 24 TUILES

RECIPE NOTE

To achieve the classic tuile shape, the wafer must be shaped on a curved surface while still hot.

Preheat the oven to 350°F (180°C). Butter a large sheet pan.

In a food processor, combine the ½ cup (60 g) pecans and the sugar and process until finely ground. Transfer to a bowl. Stir in the flour, followed by the butter, egg whites, and vanilla, and mix well.

Working in batches, spoon the batter by heaping teaspoonfuls onto the prepared pan, spacing the mounds at least 3 inches (7.5 cm) apart. Using an icing spatula or a dinner knife, spread each mound into a round 2½ inches (6 cm) in diameter. Sprinkle each round with a generous ½ teaspoon of the chopped pecans.

Bake the cookies until the edges are darkly golden and the centers are lightly golden, about 9 minutes. Using a thin, flexible metal spatula and working quickly, lift each tuile from the sheet pan and drape it over a rolling pin. Let cool until firm, about 1 minute, then carefully transfer to a wire rack to cool completely. If the tuiles cool too much on the pan and become brittle, return the pan to the oven briefly to soften them. Repeat with the remaining batter and chopped pecans, always allowing the pan to cool before buttering it for the next batch.

CANELÉS

A specialty of Bordeaux, *canelés* are believed to have first been baked by nuns in the city's Convent of the Annonciades about three hundred years ago. The small cakes—rich and moist on the inside, dark brown on the outside—largely disappeared after the French Revolution due to the forced closure of the pastry guild devoted to their production. They resurfaced in French pastry shops in the early twentieth century, however, and soon became an elegant teatime treat in neighboring Britain.

2¼ cups (525 ml) milk

1 vanilla bean, split lengthwise

2 whole eggs

2 egg yolks

1¼ cups (250 g) sugar

1 cup (125 g) plus 2 tablespoons flour

4 tablespoons (60 g) unsalted butter, melted, plus 2 tablespoons, melted, for the molds

1 tablespoon light rum

MAKES 15–18 PASTRIES

Pour the milk into a saucepan. Using the tip of a knife, scrape the seeds from the vanilla bean into the milk, then add the pod halves. Place over medium-high heat and heat until small bubbles appear along the edges of the pan, about 5 minutes. Remove from the heat and let cool to warm.

In a small bowl, whisk the whole eggs until blended. In another small bowl, whisk the egg yolks until blended. In a large bowl, whisk together the sugar and flour. Make a well in the center of the flour mixture, add the whole eggs and then the egg yolks to the well, and whisk to create a thick paste. Remove the vanilla pod from the milk and discard. Add the warm milk, melted butter, and rum to the egg mixture and whisk until well blended. Cover the bowl with plastic wrap and refrigerate for at least 1 hour or up to 2 hours.

Preheat the oven to 350°F (180°C). Using a pastry brush, brush canelé molds with some of the remaining 2 tablespoons melted butter and refrigerate for 15 minutes. (If you do not have canelé molds, butter 12 standard muffin cups using all the butter.)

Stir the batter well, then fill each chilled mold (or muffin cup) almost to the rim. Place the molds on a sheet pan. Bake the canelés until they are dark brown and puffed on the edges with a slight depression in the center, about 1 hour; do not open the oven door during baking. Remove the canelés from the oven and unmold them onto a wire rack while they are still hot. Continue buttering, chilling, and filling the molds and baking the canelés until all of the batter has been used, always refrigerating the batter between batches.

Serve the canelés warm or at room temperature.

CHELSEA BUNS

Introduced in the early 1700s at the Chelsea Bun House in South West London, this currant bun, made famous by proprietor Richard Hand—aka Captain Bun—became the must-have treat for that era and beyond. The royal family was known to be such avid fans of the square, fruit-filled yeasted bun that the bakery was nicknamed the Royal Bun House.

FOR THE DOUGH

3 cups (375 g) flour

3 tablespoons sugar

2 teaspoons quick-rise yeast

1 teaspoon salt

1 cup (240 ml) whole milk, warmed (115°–125°F/45°–52°C)

4 tablespoons (60 g) unsalted butter, melted

Nonstick cooking spray or neutral oil, for the bowl

FOR THE FILLING

3 tablespoons sugar

2 teaspoons mixed spice or pumpkin pie spice

3 tablespoons unsalted butter, melted

1 cup (140 g) dried currants

FOR THE GLAZE

¼ cup (50 g) granulated sugar

2 tablespoons very hot tap water

MAKES 9 BUNS

To make the dough, in the bowl of a stand mixer, whisk together the flour, sugar, yeast, and salt, then fit the mixer with the dough hook. Turn the mixer on medium-low speed, pour the milk and butter into the flour mixture, and beat until the flour is completely incorporated. Increase the speed to medium and beat until the dough is shiny and pulls away from the bottom of the bowl, 8–10 minutes. If the dough climbs up the hook, stop the mixer and scrape down the dough into the bowl.

Transfer the dough to a work surface, knead once or twice until it no longer sticks to the surface, and shape into a ball. Lightly grease the sides of the mixer bowl, then put the dough back into the bowl. Cover the bowl with a plate or plastic wrap, place in a warm spot, and let the dough rise until doubled in size, about 1 hour.

Lightly grease a 9-inch (23-cm) square baking pan with 2-inch (5-cm) sides. (For the best results, use a straight-sided pan.) To make the filling, in a small bowl, whisk together the sugar and mixed spice until well blended. Set aside along with the butter and currants.

Recipe continues on the following page

VIOLET: *Ah. Just the ticket. Nanny always said sweet tea was the thing for frayed nerves. Though why it has to be sweet I couldn't tell you.*

~ SEASON 1, EPISODE 3

Continued

To shape and fill the buns, scrape the dough out onto a work surface (no flour needed) and press down on it to deflate it. Using your hands or a rolling pin, shape the dough into a 9 x 18-inch (23 x 46-cm) rectangle, with a short side facing you. Pour the melted butter into the center of the dough rectangle and, using an offset spatula, spread it evenly to the edges. Sprinkle the sugar mixture evenly over the butter. Scatter the currants on top and press gently into the dough.

Roll up the dough Swiss roll–style and pinch to seal the seam. Position the roll, seam side down, on the work surface and reshape it into a log about 9 inches (23 cm) long. Using a serrated knife, trim off the ends, then cut the log into 9 slices each 1 inch (2.5 cm) thick. Arrange the slices, with a cut side down, in three rows in the prepared pan.

Loosely but completely cover the baking pan with storage wrap and place in a warm spot. Let the buns rise until they are puffed, fill the pan, and have taken on a square appearance, about 1 hour. About 40 minutes into the rising, preheat the oven to 350°F (180°C).

Meanwhile, make the glaze. In a small bowl, stir together the sugar and water until the sugar dissolves. Set aside.

Bake the buns until they are puffed and deep golden brown, 42–45 minutes. Transfer the pan to a wire rack, spoon the glaze evenly over the buns, and let the buns cool for about 15 minutes. Serve warm.

PRINCE OF WALES BISCUITS

The original version of this confection, popular in the Regency period of the early 1800s, was a sturdy, unsweetened biscuit (aka cookie) stamped with the traditional feather emblem of the Prince. Made by commercial bakers, it was served after dinner for dunking into sweet wine. This newer, softer version is lightly sweetened and makes a delicious addition to the teatime plate. The Prince would give you permission to forgo his feathers and use any decorative stamp you like.

2⅓ cups (300 g) flour, plus more for dipping

½ teaspoon salt

¾ cup (170 g) cold unsalted butter, diced

½ cup (100 g) sugar

1 egg

1 teaspoon pure vanilla extract

MAKES ABOUT 17 BISCUITS

TEA ETIQUETTE

These biscuits have a low percentage of sugar, so don't expect browning. If you want a slightly sweeter cookie, increase the sugar amount to ⅔ cup (140 g).

Preheat the oven to 350°F (180°C). Line three sheet pans with parchment paper.

In a medium bowl, whisk together the flour and salt. In a large bowl, using an electric mixer, beat the butter on medium speed until smooth, about 1 minute. Add the sugar, increase the speed to medium-high, and beat until fluffy and lighter in color, 2–3 minutes. Add the egg and vanilla and beat until fully incorporated. On medium-low speed, add the flour mixture and beat just until blended.

Put a few spoonfuls of flour in a small, shallow bowl to use for dipping. Using your hands, shape the dough into 1½-inch (4-cm) balls each weighing about 1¼ oz (35 g)—about the size of a golf ball—and set aside on a work surface. Working with 6 dough balls at a time, dip half of each ball into the flour to coat the upper half lightly and arrange the balls, flour side up and about 3 inches (7.5 cm) apart, on a prepared pan. Lightly flour a 3-inch (7.5-cm) cookie stamp and gently but firmly flatten the dough ball until the dough reaches the edges of the stamp (any excess can be trimmed away with the tip of a knife). Carefully lift off the stamp. Repeat the flouring and pressing with the remaining dough balls, arranging them on the remaining two sheet pans.

Bake one sheet pan at a time (slide the remaining pans into the refrigerator if the kitchen is warm) until the biscuits are pale golden brown around the edges (the bottoms will be more golden brown than the edges), 15–17 minutes. Let the biscuits cool on the pan on a wire rack for 10 minutes, then serve. The biscuits are best when served the same day.

RASPBERRY MERINGUES

French chef François Massialot, father of the crème brûlée, published the first meringue recipe in *Nouveau cuisinier royal et bourgeois*, his multivolume cookbook that began appearing in 1691. Large, featherlight meringue shells, usually filled with raspberries and topped with cream, are a favorite sweet course on the Downton dining table. Piping meringue into small nests yields an ideal adaptation for afternoon tea.

FOR THE MERINGUE

2 egg whites

1 teaspoon fresh lemon juice

½ cup plus 1 tablespoon (115 g) superfine sugar

FOR THE FOOL

½ lb (225 g) raspberries

½ cup plus 2 tablespoons (150 ml) heavy cream

¼ cup (50 g) superfine sugar

Confectioners' sugar, if needed

Raspberries, for serving

MAKES 6 MERINGUES

To make the meringue, preheat the oven to 200°F (95°C). Line a sheet pan with parchment paper.

In a bowl, using a whisk or a handheld mixer on medium speed, beat together the egg whites and lemon juice until soft peaks form, increasing the mixer speed to medium-high once the whites are foamy and begin to thicken. While beating constantly, add the superfine sugar, a little at a time, and beat until stiff peaks form.

Fit a piping bag with a large star tip, spoon the whipped egg whites into the bag, and secure closed. Pipe 6 meringue nests each 2–3 inches (5–7.5 cm) in diameter—first outlining them, then filling the centers, and finally building up the sides—and some small stars for garnish on the prepared pan.

Bake the meringues for 2–2½ hours. They should be crisp to the touch and lift off the parchment easily. Let cool completely.

To make the fool, in a food processor or blender, purée the raspberries, then pass the purée through a fine-mesh sieve to remove the seeds. Alternatively, use a food mill to purée the berries, which will extract the seeds as it purées. (Removing the seeds is optional but would have been done in houses like Downton.)

In a bowl, using a whisk or a handheld mixer on medium speed, whip together the cream and superfine sugar until soft peaks form. Using a rubber spatula, gently fold the raspberry purée into the whipped cream just until no white streaks remain.

MRS. PATMORE: *Now, what else can I give you? Another cup of tea, why not?*

MASON: *I don't mind if I do.*

~ SEASON 6, EPISODE 5

Taste and adjust with confectioners' sugar if you prefer it sweeter. The fool should be fairly tart, however, to contrast with the meringue.

Just before serving, fill the meringue nests with the fool and top with the small star meringues. Serve with a small cluster of raspberries alongside.

CRUMPETS

Originally a thin cake cooked on a hot griddle, the crumpet, a regular feature on both the afternoon tea tray and morning breakfast table, likely owes its name and its ancestry to the dry, dense fourteenth-century crompid cake. Elizabeth Raffald introduced the soft, spongy, crater-topped modern crumpet in her 1769 book *The Experienced English Housekeeper,* dubbing it a pikelet, a term still in use for the crumpet in parts of northern England.

3¼ cups (405 g) flour

4 teaspoons salt

½ teaspoon baking soda

2 cups (480 ml) milk, 1 cup (240 ml) heated to 115°F (46°C) and 1 cup (240 ml) at room temperature

2 tablespoons sugar

1 teaspoon active dry yeast

Unsalted butter, for the molds, pan, and serving

Jam, for serving

MAKES 12 CRUMPETS

In a medium bowl, whisk together the flour, salt, and baking soda. In a large bowl, if using a handheld mixer, or in the bowl of a stand mixer, combine the heated milk, sugar, and yeast and let stand until foamy, about 10 minutes. On low speed, slowly add the flour mixture and then the room-temperature milk, beating until a smooth, thick batter forms. Cover the bowl loosely with plastic wrap and set in a warm place until the batter expands and becomes bubbly, about 1 hour.

Heat a 12-inch (30-cm) cast-iron frying pan over medium heat. While the pan is heating, butter as many 4-inch (10-cm) ring molds as will fit comfortably in the pan. When the pan is hot, lightly grease it with butter, then place the prepared molds in the pan. Fill each ring with about ⅓ cup (80 ml) batter and cook until bubbles appear on the surface, about 6 minutes. Carefully remove the rings and flip the crumpets over. Cook until the crumpets are golden on the second side and cooked through, about 5 minutes. Transfer to a plate and keep warm.

Repeat with the remaining batter, buttering the ring molds each time. Serve hot with butter and jam.

ÉCLAIRS

Éclairs appear at Downton at the end of season 6 in one of the more eventful episodes. As Mary worries about accepting Henry Talbot, Edith's latest love affair seems to have ended in disaster, Thomas is recovering from his suicide attempt, and Mrs. Patmore's Bed and Breakfast is embroiled in scandal. Amid all this, it's something of a relief to see Daisy busy filling choux pastry with custard. Éclairs and their cousins, profiteroles, originated at the turn of the nineteenth century but didn't become popular for decades.

FOR THE PASTRY CREAM

1½ cups (350 ml) milk

1 vanilla bean, split lengthwise

4 egg yolks

½ cup (100 g) sugar

2 tablespoons cornstarch

2 tablespoons unsalted butter

FOR THE CHOUX PASTRY

½ cup (120 ml) milk

½ cup (120 ml) water

6 tablespoons (90 g) unsalted butter, cut into ½-inch (12-mm) pieces

¼ teaspoon salt

1 cup (125 g) flour

4 eggs

FOR THE GANACHE

4 oz (115 g) bittersweet or semisweet chocolate, coarsely chopped

4 tablespoons (60g) unsalted butter, cut into ½-inch (12-mm) pieces

¼ cup (60 ml) milk or freshly brewed strong coffee

MAKES 10 PASTRIES

To make the pastry cream, pour the milk into a saucepan. Using the tip of a knife, scrape the seeds from the vanilla bean into the milk, then add the pod halves. Place over medium heat and heat until small bubbles appear along the edges of the pan. Remove from the heat and remove the vanilla pod.

In a bowl, whisk together the egg yolks, sugar, and cornstarch until smooth. While whisking constantly, slowly add the hot milk to the egg yolk mixture until blended. Pour the blended mixture back into the saucepan and place over medium-low heat. Cook, whisking constantly, until the mixture comes to a boil and thickens, about 3 minutes. Continue cooking, whisking constantly, for 1 minute longer. Pour through a fine-mesh sieve into a clean bowl. Add the butter and stir until melted and the mixture is smooth. Cover the bowl with storage wrap, pressing it directly onto the surface of the cream to prevent a skin from forming, then poke a few holes in the plastic with the tip of a knife to allow steam to escape. Refrigerate until well chilled, at least 2 hours or up to 2 days.

To make the choux pastry, combine the milk, water, butter, and salt in a saucepan over medium-high heat and bring to a full boil. When the butter melts, remove the pan from the heat, add the flour all at once, and stir vigorously with a wooden spoon until blended.

Return the pan to medium heat and continue stirring until the mixture leaves the sides of the pan and forms a ball. Remove from the heat and let cool for 3–4 minutes, or until cooled to 140°F (60°C) on an instant-read thermometer.

Recipe continues on the following page

Continued

TEA HISTORY

The rotund Brown Betty is an iconic British teapot made from red clay found in Staffordshire and finished with a brown manganese glaze. Pots made from the clay were prized as early as the seventeenth century because they retained heat particularly well, and the round shape, introduced early in the nineteenth century, allowed the leaves to move freely, yielding particularly flavorful tea. A taller version of the pot can often be seen in Daisy's hands when she is serving tea to the rest of the downstairs staff (see page 47). Brown Betty teapots are still made today.

Meanwhile, in a small bowl, whisk 1 egg. When the batter has cooled, pour the egg into the batter and beat with the spoon until incorporated. Add the remaining 3 eggs, one at a time, whisking each one first in the small bowl and then mixing it into the batter. After each egg is added, the mixture will separate and appear shiny, but it will return to a smooth paste with vigorous beating. Let the paste cool for about 10 minutes before shaping.

Position two racks evenly spaced in the center of the oven and preheat the oven to 425°F (220°C). Line two sheet pans with parchment paper or aluminum foil.

To shape the éclair shells, fit a piping bag with a ¾-inch (2-cm) plain tip, spoon the dough into the bag, and secure closed. Pipe out logs 4 inches (10 cm) long and 1 inch (2.5 cm) wide onto the prepared pans, spacing the logs at least 2 inches (5 cm) apart to allow for expansion.

Bake the logs for 15 minutes, then reduce the heat to 375°F (190°C) and continue baking until golden brown, 15–20 minutes longer. Remove from the oven and immediately prick the side of each log with the tip of a sharp knife. Return the pans to the oven, leave the oven door ajar, and allow the pastries to dry out for 10–15 minutes. Remove from the oven once again and let the pastries cool completely on the pans on wire racks before filling.

To make the ganache, combine the chocolate and butter in a heatproof bowl. In a small saucepan over medium-high heat, bring the milk to a boil. Remove the milk from the heat and immediately pour it over the chocolate and butter, then whisk until the chocolate and butter melt and are smooth. Transfer the ganache to a wide bowl.

Using a sharp serrated knife, cut each log in half lengthwise. One at a time, hold the top half of each pastry upside down and dip the top surface into the ganache. Turn the dipped half right side up, place on a wire rack, and let stand until set, about 15 minutes.

Fit a piping bag with a ¾-inch (2-cm) plain or star tip, spoon the pastry cream into the bag, and secure closed. Pipe the cream into the bottom half of each log. Set the ganache-topped half on top of the cream. Serve at once, or refrigerate for up to 2 hours before serving.

RASPBERRY MACARONS

John Murrell's *A Daily Exercise for Ladies and Gentlewomen,* published in London in 1617, includes a recipe for the French *macaron,* a small, sweet confection made from Jordan almonds, rose water, sugar, egg whites, and ambergris. But more than two centuries would pass before French bakers began sandwiching a filling between two meringue-based macarons, creating the *macaron parisien* popular today.

1⅓ cups (145 g) superfine almond flour

2 cups (225 g) confectioners' sugar

3 large egg whites

½ teaspoon pure vanilla extract

½ teaspoon pure almond extract

Pinch of salt

3 drops rose-pink gel paste food coloring, plus more if needed

½ cup (140 g) seedless raspberry jam

MAKES ABOUT 25 MACARONS

Line two sheet pans with parchment paper. Combine the almond flour and 1 cup (115 g) of the confectioners' sugar in a sifter or fine-mesh sieve and reserve.

In a large bowl, using an electric mixer, beat together the egg whites, vanilla and almond extracts, and salt on medium speed until soft peaks form, about 3 minutes. Increase the speed to high and gradually beat in the remaining 1 cup (110 g) confectioners' sugar, beating until stiff peaks form. Add the food coloring and beat until fully incorporated, adding more if needed to achieve the desired shade of pink.

Sift about one-fourth of the almond-sugar mixture over the beaten whites. Using a rubber spatula, fold it in until blended. Repeat with the remaining almond-sugar mixture in three equal batches, folding until incorporated and the batter flows like lava.

Fit a piping bag with a ⅜-inch (1-cm) plain tip, spoon the batter into the bag, and secure closed. Holding the piping bag with the tip about ½ inch (12 mm) above a prepared sheet pan, pipe about 25 mounds, each 1½–1¾ inches (4–4.5 cm) in diameter, onto each sheet pan, spacing the mounds about 1 inch (2.5 cm) apart. Make the mounds as smooth as possible, moving the bag off to one side after each mound is piped. Tap each sheet firmly against the work surface two or three times to release any air bubbles, then let stand at room temperature for 30–45 minutes.

Position a rack in the lower third of the oven and preheat the oven to 325°F (165°C). Bake one sheet pan at a time, rotating the pan back to front halfway through baking, until the macarons have risen

ETIQUETTE NOTE

So the Crawley family could serve themselves, a grand-looking silver tea urn filled
with hot water for replenishing the teapot was placed in the drawing room.

and just set but not browned, 10–11 minutes. The bottom of each
macaron should be dry and firm to the touch. Transfer the macarons
to a wire rack and let cool completely.

Turn half of the macarons bottom side up on a work surface and
spoon about ½ teaspoon jam onto each bottom. Top them with
the remaining macarons, bottom side down. Arrange the macarons
in a single layer on a sheet pan, cover with rstorage wrap, and
refrigerate for at least 1 day or up to 3 days before serving. Serve
chilled or at cool room temperature.

CAKES, TARTS
& PUDDINGS

BATTENBERG CAKE

Also known as a domino cake or church window cake, this almond-flavored checkerboard-style confection was named in honor of the 1884 marriage of Queen Victoria's granddaughter Victoria to Prince Louis of Battenberg. Because of anti-German sentiment in Britain during World War I, the Prince gave up his German name and dynastic titles in 1917 and took an English name, Mountbatten (the surname of the current Prince Philip of England, his grandson).

FOR THE CAKE

¾ cup (170 g) unsalted butter, at room temperature, plus more for the pan and foil

1⅓ cups (170 g) all-purpose flour, plus more for the pan and foil

⅓ cup (40 g) almond flour

1 teaspoon baking powder

½ teaspoon salt

1 cup (200 g) granulated sugar

3 eggs, at room temperature

¾ teaspoon pure vanilla extract

½ teaspoon pure almond extract

¼ cup (60 ml) milk

1–3 drops red or pink food coloring

FOR ASSEMBLY

⅓ cup (105 g) apricot jam

Confectioners' sugar, for dusting

1 tube (7 oz/198 g) marzipan (preferably white)

SERVES 8–10

To make the cake, preheat the oven to 325°F (165°C). Lightly butter the bottom and sides of an 8-inch (20-cm) square cake pan with 2-inch (5-cm) sides. Cut an 8 x 12-inch (20 x 30-cm) rectangle of aluminum foil. Fold it in half crosswise to create an 8 x 6-inch (20 x 15-cm) rectangle. Fold both ends toward the centerfold to make an edge 2 inches (5 cm) high from the center. Crease the edges of the folds (top and both bottom) firmly and unfold the sides. It will look like an upside-down T. Arrange the foil sheet in the greased pan (the center fold will divide the pan into two separate sections each 8 by 4 inches/20 by 10 cm). Lightly butter the foil and flour the sides of the pan and the foil.

In a bowl, whisk together the all-purpose flour, almond flour, baking powder, and salt. In a large bowl, using an electric mixer, beat the butter on medium speed until smooth, about 1 minute. Increase the speed to medium-high, add the granulated sugar, and beat until fluffy and lighter in color, 2–3 minutes. Add the eggs, one at a time, beating well after each addition and adding the vanilla and almond extracts along with the final egg. On low speed, add about half of the flour mixture and mix just until blended, then add the milk and again mix until blended. Add the remaining flour and mix just until blended.

Divide the batter in half (about 14 oz/400 g each). Scrape half of the batter into one side of the divided pan and spread evenly. Add 1 drop of the food coloring to the remaining batter and fold until evenly colored, adding more food coloring as needed to achieve the pink intensity desired. Scrape the pink batter into the other side of the pan and spread evenly.

Recipe continues on the following page

Bake the cakes until a toothpick inserted into the center of each side comes out clean, 32–34 minutes. Let cool in the pan on a wire rack for about 15 minutes. Run a thin-bladed knife around the inside of the pan to loosen the cake sides. Invert a rack on top of the pan and, using pot holders, grip the pan and the rack and invert together. Gently lift off the pan, peel away the foil, and let the cakes cool completely.

To assemble the cake, in a small saucepan, warm the jam over low heat until fluid, then pass it through a fine-mesh sieve set over a small bowl, pressing on the solids.

Place a cake, top side up, on a work surface. Using a serrated knife, cut away the domed top to level the cake. Trim the four sides to make them even, then measure the height of the cake (about 1¼ inches/3 cm). Using a ruler, cut the layer lengthwise into 2 strips that are the same width as the height of the cake. You should now have 2 strips of equal height and width. Repeat with the remaining cake, leveling the top and cutting into 2 strips. You should now have 4 strips of equal height and width. Trim all 4 strips to equal length (about 7 inches/18 cm long).

Lightly dust a work surface with confectioners' sugar. Place the marzipan on the dusted surface and, using a rolling pin, roll out the marzipan into an 8 x 11½-inch (20 x 29-cm) rectangle. Lightly dust with more confectioners' sugar if the marzipan is sticky. Trim off the edges to make a 7 x 10½-inch (18 x 26.5-cm) rectangle.

Arrange the marzipan with a long side facing you. Using an offset spatula, spread a thin layer of the jam crosswise down the center 5 inches (13 cm) of the marzipan. Arrange a pink cake strip on the left side on top of the jam, pressing gently. Spread a thin layer of the jam over the inside edge of the cake strip and arrange a plain cake strip next to it. Gently press the strips together. Spread a thin layer of jam over the tops of the strips and repeat with the remaining strips and jam, stacking the cake strips in reverse order like a checkerboard.

Spread a thin coating of jam over the top and sides of the stacked strips. Lift one side of the marzipan over the cake, pressing gently to adhere to the side. Using a fingertip, brush a little water over the marzipan edge on the top of the cake. Repeat with the other side of the marzipan, again pressing gently against the side of the cake and then pressing on the overlapping portion of the marzipan to seal the edges. Turn the cake over so the seam is on the bottom and then wrap in storage wrap. Refrigerate for at least 1 hour or up to 3 days.

Serve chilled or at room temperature, cut into slices.

ORANGE BUTTER CAKES

Sweet oranges were largely unknown in Europe until the fifteenth and sixteenth centuries, when Italian and Portuguese merchants encouraged their cultivation in the Mediterranean area. But they would not be widely available in the cold climes of northern Europe until the nineteenth century, when newly established rail systems began transporting fresh foods. British bakers, who had long been fond of uniting plain cake with fresh fruit, might well have turned out these little teatime cakes, each topped with a thin orange slice, to celebrate this latest addition to their larder.

6 tablespoons (90 g) unsalted butter, melted and cooled, plus ½ cup (115 g) and more for the ramekins, at room temperature

2 oranges

¾ cup (155 g) firmly packed light brown sugar

1 cup (125 g) flour

1 teaspoon baking powder

½ teaspoon baking soda

¼ teaspoon salt

½ cup (100 g) granulated sugar

2 eggs, at room temperature

¼ cup (60 ml) heavy cream, at room temperature

1 teaspoon pure vanilla extract

MAKES 6 SMALL CAKES

Preheat the oven to 350°F (180°C). Lightly butter six 1-cup (240-ml) ramekins or custard cups.

Grate the zest of 1 orange; reserve the fruit for another use. Cut the second orange crosswise into 6 very thin slices; you may not need the whole orange.

Sprinkle 2 tablespoons of the brown sugar onto the bottom of each prepared ramekin. Pour 1 tablespoon of the melted butter into each ramekin, evenly covering the sugar. Place 1 orange slice in each ramekin. Place the ramekins on a sheet pan.

Sift together the flour, baking powder, baking soda, and salt into a small bowl. In a large bowl, using an electric mixer, beat the remaining ½ cup (115 g) butter on medium speed until smooth, about 1 minute. Increase the speed to medium-high, add the granulated sugar and orange zest, and beat until fluffy and lighter in color, 3–5 minutes. Add the eggs, one at a time, beating well after each addition. Using a rubber spatula, fold in the flour mixture until well blended. Add the cream and vanilla and stir until thoroughly incorporated.

Divide the batter evenly among the ramekins, spooning it over the orange slices. Bake the cakes until the tops are golden and a toothpick inserted into the center of a cake comes out clean, about 35 minutes. Let the ramekins cool on the pan on a wire rack for 10 minutes.

Recipe continues on the following page

Continued

Run a thin-bladed knife around the edge of each ramekin to loosen the cake sides. Working with 1 cake at a time, invert a small dessert plate over the ramekin, then invert the ramekin and plate together in a single quick motion. Lightly tap the bottom of the ramekin with the knife handle to loosen the cake, then lift off the ramekin. If an orange slice sticks to a ramekin, loosen it with the knife tip and replace it on the cake. Serve the cakes warm or at room temperature.

GINGER BUTTER CAKE

Believed to have originated in Southeast Asia, ginger was a highly coveted import to the Roman Empire. It was already widely available in England in Anglo-Saxon times, and by the late Middle Ages, it was almost as common as pepper and was added to all manner of dishes. Since the eighteenth century, its culinary use has been primarily limited to baked goods, such as this simple teatime cake.

¾ cup (170 g) unsalted butter, at room temperature, plus more for the pan

2 cups (250 g) cake flour, plus more for the pan

¾ cup (130 g) chopped crystallized ginger, minced

⅓ cup (80 ml) Grand Marnier or other orange liqueur

2 teaspoons baking powder

2 teaspoons ground ginger

1¼ cups (140 g) confectioners' sugar, sifted, plus more for dusting

1 tablespoon light corn syrup

4 eggs

Grated zest of 1 orange

3-inch (7.5-cm) piece fresh ginger, peeled and grated

½ teaspoon pure almond extract

½ cup (120 ml) milk

SERVES 8

Preheat the oven to 350°F (180°C). Butter the bottom and sides of a 9 x 5 x 3-inch (23 x 13 x 7.5-cm) loaf pan, then dust with flour, tapping out the excess.

In a small bowl, combine the crystallized ginger and Grand Marnier and let stand for 10 minutes. Sift together the flour, baking powder, and ground ginger into a bowl.

In a large bowl, using an electric mixer, beat the butter on medium speed until smooth, about 1 minute. Increase the speed to medium-high, add the sifted confectioners' sugar and corn syrup, and beat until fluffy and lighter in color, 4–5 minutes. Add the eggs, one at a time, beating well after each addition. Add the orange zest, fresh ginger, and almond extract and beat until blended.

Using a rubber spatula, gently fold in one-third of the flour mixture until almost fully incorporated. Fold in half of the milk, followed by half of the remaining flour mixture and then the remaining milk. Add the remaining flour mixture and the liqueur-soaked crystallized ginger and fold in just until the batter is smooth and the flour mixture is fully incorporated. Do not overmix or the cake will be tough.

Transfer the batter to the prepared pan, spread evenly, and smooth the top. Bake the cake until a toothpick inserted into the center comes out clean, 50–60 minutes. Let cool in the pan on a wire rack for at least 5 minutes, then turn the cake out onto the rack and turn the cake right side up. Lightly dust the top with confectioners' sugar just before serving. Serve warm or at room temperature.

MINI VICTORIA SPONGE CAKES

Also known as a Victoria sandwich, the Queen's actual teatime sponge cake would have been sandwiched with only a thick layer of raspberry jam and topped with a sprinkle of sugar. The earliest recipe for this buttery vanilla-infused cake appeared in *Mrs. Beeton's Household Management*, published in London in 1861. The addition of a layer of whipped cream or buttercream is a recent innovation but one the Grantham family would likely have enjoyed.

FOR THE CAKE

1 cup (225 g) unsalted butter, at room temperature, plus more for the ramekins

2 cups (250 g) flour, plus more for the ramekins

1½ teaspoons baking powder

½ teaspoon salt

1 cup (200 g) granulated sugar

4 large eggs, at room temperature

2 teaspoons pure vanilla extract

FOR THE FILLING

1¼ cups (300 ml) heavy cream

2 tablespoons confectioners' sugar

⅔ cup (210 g) strawberry or raspberry jam

Confectioners' sugar, for dusting

MAKES 12 SMALL CAKES

To make the cake, put an 11 x 17-inch (29 x 43-cm) sheet pan in the oven and preheat the oven to 350°F (180°C). Lightly butter the bottom and sides of twelve ¾-cup (180-ml) straight-sided ramekins or a 12-cup mini sandwich pan.

In a small bowl, whisk together the flour, baking powder, and salt. In a large bowl, using an electric mixer, beat the butter on medium speed until smooth, about 1 minute. Add the granulated sugar, increase the speed to medium-high, and beat until fluffy and lighter in color, 2–3 minutes. Add the eggs, one at a time, beating well after each addition and adding the vanilla along with the final egg. On low speed, add the flour mixture and mix just until blended.

Divide the batter evenly among the ramekins or mini sandwich cups (a slightly rounded ¼ cup/60 ml each) and spread evenly. Transfer the ramekins or mini sandwich pan to the sheet pan and bake until a toothpick inserted into the center of a cake or two comes out clean, 17–19 minutes.

Transfer the sheet pan to a wire rack and let the cakes cool for 15 minutes. Run a thin-bladed knife around the inside of each ramekin to loosen the cake sides, then invert the ramekin onto a wire rack, lift it off, and turn the cake right side up. If using a mini sandwich pan, loosen the cake sides the same way, then invert the pan onto a rack, lift off the pan, and turn the cakes right side up. (If the cups have a removable bottom, push up to release the cakes.) Let the cakes cool completely.

Recipe continues on the following page

HISTORY NOTE

The Victoria sponge
was made possible
by the invention of
baking powder by
British chemist
Alfred Bird in 1843.
A favorite of Queen
Victoria, it soon became
the iconic cake to serve
guests with tea.

Continued

While the cakes are cooling, ready the filling. In a bowl, using a handheld mixer, beat together the cream and confectioners' sugar on medium speed until stiff peaks form, 2–3 minutes. Fit a piping bag with a small plain or star tip, spoon the whipped cream into the bag, and secure closed. Use right away or refrigerate for up to 2 hours before serving.

Just before serving, using a serrated knife, cut the cakes in half horizontally. Arrange the bottom halves, cut side up, on a work surface. Divide the whipped cream evenly among the cake bottoms, piping small dollops around the edge and then into the center, covering the bottom completely. Spoon about 1 tablespoon of the jam over the cream on each cake bottom, gently spreading it to the edge. Arrange the cake tops, cut side down, on top of the jam. Lightly dust the top of each cake with confectioners' sugar.

MADEIRA CAKE

Popular in the mid-nineteenth century and into the twentieth century, Madeira cake is named for the fortified Portuguese wine that traditionally accompanied it. The wine's taste notes of toasted nuts, caramel, and fruit pair well with the subtle lemon flavor of the cake. Both the wine, often served in a cut-crystal decanter, and the cake, would have been common additions to the Downton tea table.

½ cup (115 g) unsalted butter, melted and cooled, plus room-temperature butter for the pan

¾ cup plus 2 tablespoons (170 g) superfine sugar, plus more for the pan

1 cup (125 g) flour

Grated zest of 1 large or 2 small lemons

½ teaspoon baking powder

3 eggs

½ teaspoon pure vanilla extract

SERVES 8

Preheat the oven to 350°F (180°C). Butter an 8½ x 4½ x 2½-inch (21.5 x 11.5 x 6-cm) loaf pan, then lightly coat with sugar, tapping out the excess.

In a small bowl, whisk together the flour, lemon zest, and baking powder. In a separate, larger bowl, whisk the eggs until thick and creamy. Slowly add the sugar, whisking constantly until fully incorporated. Continuing to whisk constantly, very slowly add the melted butter just until incorporated. (Alternatively, use a handheld mixer on medium-high speed to beat the eggs, then beat in the sugar, and finally the butter.) Carefully fold in the flour mixture just until combined.

Pour the batter into the prepared pan, then get the pan into the oven quickly, before the eggs have a chance to collapse. Bake the cake until a toothpick inserted into the center comes out clean, about 30 minutes. Let cool in the pan on a wire rack for 10 minutes, then carefully turn the cake out onto the rack, turn the cake right side up, and let cool completely before serving.

SIMNEL CAKE

The name of this cake likely derives from the Latin *simla*, which was a flour grade available in ancient Rome used for making a yeast-leavened bread. By the Middle Ages, simnel cake was linked to the Easter holiday, and by the twentieth century, it had evolved into a light fruitcake accented with marzipan, both as a layer inside the cake and for decoration. In this regional adaptation, the cake is topped with a fluted marzipan round and eleven balls symbolizing the apostles of Jesus.

FOR THE MARZIPAN

2¼ cups (225 g) ground almonds

1 cup plus 2 tablespoons (225 g) superfine sugar

1 egg, lightly whisked

1 teaspoon orange flower water

1 teaspoon fresh lemon juice

1 teaspoon apricot or hazelnut schnapps

FOR THE CAKE

½ cup plus 2 tablespoons (145 g) salted butter, at room temperature, plus more for the pan

1¾ cups plus 2 tablespoons (235 g) flour, plus more for the work surface

2 teaspoons ground ginger

½ teaspoon ground cinnamon

½ teaspoon baking powder

¾ cup (150 g) superfine sugar

4 eggs

⅓ cup (80 ml) milk

1½ cups (210 g) dried currants

¼ lb (115 g) dried apricots, chopped

¼ lb (115 g) mixed candied orange and lemon peel, chopped

1 teaspoon grated lemon zest

1 teaspoon grated orange zest

SERVES 12–14

To make the marzipan, in a bowl, combine the ground almonds, sugar, egg, orange flower water, lemon juice, and schnapps and stir together until all the ingredients are well blended and a soft, pliable consistency forms that can be rolled out. Enclose in storage wrap and refrigerate until ready to use.

To make the cake, preheat the oven to 350°F (180°C). Butter the bottom and sides of an 8-inch (20-cm) round cake pan, then line the bottom and sides with a double layer of parchment paper and butter the paper generously.

In a bowl, whisk together the flour, ginger, cinnamon, and baking powder. In a large bowl, using an electric mixer, beat the butter on medium speed until smooth, about 1 minute. Increase the speed to medium-high, add the sugar, and beat until fluffy and lighter in color, 2–3 minutes. On medium speed, add the eggs, one at a time, alternately with the flour mixture in three batches, beginning and ending with the eggs and beating well after each addition. Beat in the milk until blended. Using a wooden spoon, stir in the currants, apricots, candied citrus peel, and citrus zests until evenly distributed.

Divide the marzipan into thirds. On a lightly floured work surface, roll out one-third of the marzipan into an 8-inch (20-cm) round (the diameter of the pan). Pour half of the batter into the prepared pan. Carefully lay the marzipan round on top of the batter in the pan, then pour the remaining batter over the marzipan layer and smooth the top.

Recipe continues on the following page

ATTICUS: *You must have a very sweet tooth.*

She laughs.

ROSE: *No, they're not for me. I give tea to some Russian refugees every Tuesday and Thursday. They love cake.*

ATTICUS: *I love cake!*

~ SEASON 5, EPISODE 5

Continued

RECIPE NOTE

For a shortcut, substitute 18 oz (500 g) store-bought marzipan for the homemade.

Bake the cake until a toothpick inserted into the center of the top cake layer (not to the marzipan) comes out clean, about 2 hours. Keep an eye on the top, and if it starts to brown too much, cover it loosely with aluminum foil. Let cool in the pan on a wire rack for 10–15 minutes, then invert the pan onto the rack, lift off the pan, and peel off the parchment. Turn the cake right side up and let cool completely.

If the cake has a domed top, using a serrated knife and a sawing motion, cut off the dome to make the top level, then set the cake on a serving plate. Divide the remaining marzipan in half. Using a rolling pin, roll out half of the marzipan into a 10-inch (25-cm) round and lay the round on top of the cake. Using a thumb and two index fingers, flute the edge of the marzipan round decoratively. Divide the remaining marzipan into 11 equal pieces. Roll each piece into a ball and arrange the balls along the top edge of the cake. Using a kitchen torch, brown the top of the cake (or slip the cake briefly under a preheated broiler). Cut into wedges to serve.

BANBURY TARTS

This iconic British confection, in which a spiced dried-fruit filling is baked in a flaky, traditionally lard-based pastry shell, is an icon of British culinary history. The first known recipe for a Banbury cake appeared in *The English Huswife*, published in 1615, and called for fashioning a sweet yeasted dough and currants into a big, rather elaborate pastry. By the early nineteenth century, individual open-faced tarts featuring currants or raisins were also being made, a size and filling that has remained popular. The tarts were enjoyed across the classes and would have been served both upstairs and downstairs at Downton.

Tart Pastry (page 75)

1½ cups (255 g) raisins

1 cup (240 ml) water

⅔ cup (140 g) sugar

4 soda crackers, finely crushed

2 teaspoons grated lemon zest

2 tablespoons fresh lemon juice

1 egg, lightly whisked

MAKES TWENTY-FOUR 1½-INCH (4-CM) MINI TARTS

Make the tart pastry and refrigerate as directed.

Have ready a 24-cup mini muffin pan (cups should be about 1¾ inches / 4.5 cm in diameter and ¾ inch / 2 cm deep).

On a lightly floured work surface, roll out the dough about ⅛ inch (3 mm) thick. Using a 2½-inch (6-cm) round cutter, cut out as many rounds as possible. Transfer each round to a muffin cup, gently pressing the dough onto the bottom and up the sides. Gather up the dough scraps, press together, reroll, and cut out more rounds to line the remaining cups. Place the lined pan in the freezer until chilled, about 30 minutes. About 15 minutes before the pastry shells are ready to bake, preheat the oven to 375°F (190°C).

Using a fork, prick the bottom and sides of the pastry lining each cup. Bake until almost golden, about 10 minutes. Let cool completely on a wire rack. Leave the oven set at 375°F (190°C).

In a heavy saucepan over high heat, combine the raisins, water, sugar, crackers, and lemon zest and bring to a boil, stirring to dissolve the sugar. Reduce the heat to low and simmer uncovered, stirring occasionally, until slightly thickened, about 10 minutes. Remove from the heat and stir in the lemon juice and egg until blended.

THOMAS: *Oh, I'm worn out. Give me some tea.*

~ SEASON 6, EPISODE 1

Spoon the raisin mixture into the pastry shells, dividing it evenly and being careful not to spill any onto the pan, which could cause the pastry to stick. Bake until lightly browned on top, about 30 minutes. Remove from the oven, let cool briefly in the pan on a wire rack, and then transfer to the rack. Serve warm.

LEMON TARTS

In the late nineteenth and early twentieth century, lemon curd had a prominent place on the afternoon tea table as the preferred alternative to jam. It was a precious choice as well because, unlike jam, the egg-based curd needed refrigeration for long-term storage. Here, spooned into small, crisp tart shells, it becomes the ideal filling for a quintessential teatime offering.

FOR THE TART PASTRY

1¼ cups (155 g) flour, plus more for the work surface

3 tablespoons sugar

¼ teaspoon salt

10 tablespoons (140 g) cold unsalted butter, cut into tablespoon-size pieces

1 egg yolk

1½ tablespoons ice-cold water, or more if needed

1 cup (250 g) Lemon Curd (page 134)

Fresh berries, thin lemon slices, or edible blossoms, for garnish

Confectioners' sugar, for dusting (optional)

MAKES SIXTEEN
3-INCH (7.5-CM) TARTS

ETIQUETTE NOTE

Small cakes and tarts are often featured on the tea table in *Downton Abbey*. These bite-size treats were considered finger food, which freed guests from using a knife and fork.

To make the tart pastry, in a bowl, whisk together the flour, sugar, and salt. Scatter the butter over the flour mixture and, using your fingertips, two knives, or a pastry blender, work in the butter until the mixture forms large, coarse crumbs. In a small bowl, whisk together the egg yolk and water until blended. Add the egg mixture to the flour mixture and stir and toss gently with a fork until the flour mixture is evenly moistened and forms clumps. Feel the dough; it should be just damp enough to form a rough mass. If necessary, mix in a few more drops of water to achieve the correct consistency. Turn out the dough onto a large piece of storage wrap, cover with the wrap, and shape into a smooth disk. Refrigerate the wrapped dough at least 1 hour or up to overnight.

Have ready sixteen 3-inch (7.5-cm) tartlet pans. On a lightly floured work surface, roll out the dough about ¼ inch (6 mm) thick. Using a round pastry cutter about 3 inches (7.5 cm) in diameter, cut out as many rounds as possible. One at a time, transfer the dough rounds to the tartlet pans, gently pressing the dough onto the bottom and up the sides of each pan and trimming off any overhang. Gather up the scraps, press together, reroll, cut out more rounds, and line the remaining pans. Place the lined pans on a sheet pan and place in the freezer until well chilled, about 30 minutes. About 15 minutes before the pastry shells are ready to bake, preheat the oven to 375°F (190°C).

Using a fork, prick the bottom and sides of the pastry lining each pan. Bake the tartlet shells until golden, 12–14 minutes. Transfer to a wire rack and let cool completely.

Carefully remove the cooled tartlet shells from the pans. Fill the shells with the lemon curd, spreading it in an even layer. Garnish with the fruit or flowers, dust with confectioners' sugar (if using), and serve.

QUINCE TART

In 1275, Edward I planted four quince trees at the Tower of London, thus marking the first recorded appearance of the fragrant fruit being cultivated in England. Recipes for quince jam and jellies, pies, and tarts followed, including an elaborate lattice-top pie published in *The Whole Duty of a Woman* in 1701. At Downton, this simpler tart, in which the filling of quince slices is finished with a glaze of apricot jam, might have drawn on fruit from the estate's gardens.

Tart Pastry (page 75)
2½ cups (600 ml) water
1½ cups (300 g) sugar
1 cinnamon stick, about 2 inches (5 cm) long
1 teaspoon grated lemon zest
3 quinces
½ cup (140 g) apricot jam

SERVES 12

Make the tart pastry and refrigerate as directed.

On a lightly floured work surface, roll out the pastry into a round 12 inches (30 cm) in diameter and about ¼ inch (6 mm) thick. Roll the dough around the pin, center the pin over a 9-inch (23-cm) fluted tart pan with a removable bottom, and unroll the dough, centering it in the pan and allowing the excess to overhang the sides. Press the dough onto the bottom and up the sides of the pan, then trim the edges, allowing a ½-inch (12-mm) overhang. Roll the overhang back over onto itself and press firmly to reinforce the sides of the crust. Place the lined pan in the freezer until chilled, about 30 minutes. About 15 minutes before the tart crust is ready to bake, preheat the oven to 375°F (190°C).

Line the chilled pastry crust with parchment paper and fill with pie weights or dried beans. Bake until the crust is dry to the touch and the edges are beginning to color, about 15 minutes. Remove from the oven and remove the weights and parchment. Lower the oven temperature to 350°F (180°C), return the tart crust to the oven, and bake until golden brown all over, 10–15 minutes longer. Let cool completely in the pan on a wire rack.

To make the filling, in a saucepan over medium heat, combine the water, sugar, cinnamon stick, and lemon zest and bring to a boil, stirring until the sugar dissolves. Reduce the heat to low so the syrup simmers gently.

THOMAS: *What would my Mother say? Me entertaining the future Earl of Grantham to tea.*

MATTHEW: *War has a way of distinguishing between the things that matter, and the things that don't.*

~ SEASON 2, EPISODE 1

Peel, halve, and core each quince, then cut each half into 4 wedges. Drop the wedges into the simmering sugar syrup, cover partially, and cook until tender but not mushy, about 1 hour. Remove from the heat and let cool completely. Drain the quinces well, reserving the liquid. Pat the quinces dry.

Cut each quince wedge lengthwise into 2 or 3 slices; set aside. In a small, heavy saucepan, combine the apricot jam with ¼ cup (60 ml) of the reserved quince liquid. Place over high heat, bring to a boil, and boil until thick and syrupy, which should take several minutes. Pass the syrup through a fine-mesh sieve into a small heatproof bowl.

To unmold the cooled tart crust, place the tart pan on a can or overturned bowl and carefully slide the outer ring down. Using a wide offset spatula, loosen the crust from the pan bottom and slide it onto a serving plate.

Brush a thin coating of the warm glaze over the bottom of the cooled tart crust. Arrange the quince slices attractively in the tart crust, overlapping them. Carefully brush the fruit with the remaining glaze and serve as soon as possible.

BAKEWELL TART

This almond-and-jam-filled tart is all but a national treasure in England and is, possibly, the ultimate teatime sweet. Though it's named for the town in Derbyshire where it's likely that it was first introduced, its exact origins are unknown. You can use different jams or fruits and coat it with a sugary glaze, though if you did, Mrs. Patmore would likely call it by another name entirely.

Tart Pastry (page 75)

½ cup (115 g) unsalted butter, at room temperature, plus more for the pan

½ cup (100 g) sugar

½ teaspoon pure almond or vanilla extract (optional)

Pinch of salt

2 eggs, at room temperature

1¼ cups (140 g) almond flour

½ cup (140 g) raspberry or strawberry jam

3 tablespoons sliced almonds (optional)

SERVES 12

Make the tart pastry and refrigerate as directed.

Lightly butter the bottom and sides of a fluted 9-inch (23-cm) tart pan with a removable bottom. On a lightly floured work surface, roll out the pastry into a round 12 inches (30 cm) in diameter and about ¼ inch (6 mm) thick. Roll the dough around the pin, center the pin over the tart pan, and unroll the dough, centering it in the pan and allowing the excess to overhang the sides. Press the dough onto the bottom and up the sides of the pan, then trim the edges, allowing a ½-inch (12-mm) overhang. Roll the overhang back over onto itself and press firmly to reinforce the sides of the crust. Place the lined pan in the freezer while the oven heats, 15–20 minutes.

Preheat the oven to 350°F (180°C).

Line the chilled pastry crust with parchment paper and fill with pie weights or dried beans. Bake until the edges of the crust are light brown, about 20 minutes. Remove from the oven and remove the weights and parchment. Return to the oven and continue baking until the crust is pale golden, 7–9 minutes. Transfer the pan to a wire rack. Leave the oven set at 350°F (180°C).

To make the filling, in a bowl, using an electric mixer, beat together the butter, sugar, almond extract (if using), and salt on medium speed until fluffy and lighter in color, 2–4 minutes. Add the eggs, one at a time, beating well after each addition. On medium-low speed, add the almond flour and beat just until blended.

Recipe continues on the following page

Continued

RECIPE NOTE

The prebaked crust can
be cooled completely,
covered, and stored at
room temperature for
up to 1 day before
filling and baking.

Spread the jam evenly in the warm tart crust. Drop the filling in small scoopfuls over the jam, then spread carefully and evenly over the jam. Scatter the almonds over the top, if using. Bake the tart until the filling is puffed and browned and the center springs back when lightly pressed, 35–38 minutes. Let cool completely on a wire rack.

To serve, place the tart pan on a can or overturned bowl and carefully slide the outer ring down. Using a wide offset spatula, loosen the crust from the pan bottom and slide the tart onto a serving plate.

STICKY TOFFEE PUDDINGS

Although early British puddings were either savory (meat based) or sweet and were typically boiled in special pudding bags, modern British puddings are commonly dense, moist cakes—often laced with rehydrated dried fruits—that are either steamed or baked. These toffee-topped puddings did not appear on the English table until the late twentieth century, though similar small puddings baked in ramekins would not have been uncommon in Mrs. Patmore's kitchen.

FOR THE PUDDINGS

4 tablespoons (60 g) unsalted butter, at room temperature, plus more for the custard cups

1 cup (125 g) flour, plus more for the custard cups

½ cup (70 g) pitted and finely chopped dates

¾ teaspoon baking soda

¾ cup (180 ml) boiling water

1¼ teaspoons baking powder

½ teaspoon salt

¾ cup (155 g) firmly packed dark brown sugar

2 eggs

2 teaspoons pure vanilla extract

FOR THE SAUCE

4 tablespoons (60 g) unsalted butter

¾ cup (155 g) firmly packed dark brown sugar

¾ cup (180 ml) heavy cream

2 teaspoons pure vanilla extract

Pinch of salt

MAKES 8 PUDDINGS

To make the puddings, preheat the oven to 350°F (180°C). Butter eight ½-cup (120-ml) custard cups or ramekins, then dust with flour, tapping out the excess. Place on a sheet pan.

In a small heatproof bowl, combine the dates, baking soda, and boiling water. Let stand until cool, about 10 minutes.

In a bowl, whisk together the flour, baking powder, and salt. In a large bowl, using an electric mixer, beat together the butter and brown sugar on medium speed until smooth and lighter in color, about 3 minutes. Add the eggs, one at a time, beating well after each addition and adding the vanilla with the final egg. Add the flour mixture and stir with a wooden spoon until well blended. Add the date mixture and stir until evenly distributed. The batter will be thin. Divide the batter evenly among the prepared custard cups, filling them about two-thirds full.

Bake the puddings until they are puffed and a toothpick inserted into the center comes out clean, about 20 minutes.

Meanwhile, make the sauce. In a saucepan over medium heat, melt the butter. Add the brown sugar and cream and whisk until the sauce becomes sticky, about 5 minutes. Stir in the vanilla and salt.

When the puddings are ready, remove from the oven and let cool for 5 minutes. Run a thin-bladed knife around the inside of each custard cup to loosen the pudding sides and invert the warm puddings onto individual plates. Top each pudding with a big spoonful of the toffee sauce, letting it run down the sides and onto the plate. Serve right away.

STEAMED FIGGY PUDDING

The Forme of Cury, published circa 1390, is among England's oldest cookbooks. In it is a recipe for figgy pudding's ancestor, fygey. Along with figs and raisins, it calls for "almande blanched [and] grynde . . . water and wyne, powdour gyngur and hony clarified" to be boiled, salted, and then served. Offered at the end of a meal or at teatime, the dense steamed pudding is a true British classic, here presented in a modern version.

7 tablespoons (100 g) unsalted butter, at room temperature, plus more for the mold

1½ cups (225 g) dried figs, stemmed

½ cup (70 g) dried currants

2 cups (480 ml) water

8 slices good-quality white sandwich bread, crusts removed and bread torn into pea-size crumbs

1¼ cups (155 g) flour

½ cup (100 g) firmly packed dark brown sugar

3 eggs

1 cup (240 ml) milk

1 teaspoon pure vanilla extract

2 tablespoons chopped candied orange peel

1 tablespoon grated orange zest

FOR THE WHIPPED CREAM

1½ cups (350 ml) heavy cream

¼ cup (50 g) granulated sugar

SERVES 8–10

Butter a 1½-quart (1.5-l) steamed pudding mold.

In a small saucepan over medium-high heat, combine the figs, currants, and water and bring to a boil. Reduce the heat to low and simmer, uncovered, until the figs are tender but still hold their shape, about 20 minutes. Remove from the heat.

Using a slotted spoon, transfer the figs and currants to a bowl; reserve the cooking liquid. Cut 8–10 of the figs in half lengthwise and press them, cut side down, in a decorative pattern in the prepared mold. Chop the remaining figs.

In a medium bowl, whisk together the bread crumbs and flour. In a large bowl, using an electric mixer, beat the butter on medium speed until smooth, about 1 minute. Increase the speed to medium-high, add the brown sugar, and beat until fluffy, 2–3 minutes. Add the eggs, one at a time, beating well after each addition. Add the milk and vanilla and beat until incorporated. Switch to a rubber spatula and stir in the orange peel, orange zest, currants, and chopped figs. Still using the spatula, fold half of the flour mixture into the egg mixture just until blended, then fold in the remaining flour mixture until no dry streaks remain. Pour the batter into the prepared mold and fasten the lid.

MARY: (TO SYBIL) *Oh darling, darling, don't be such a baby. This isn't Fairyland. What did you think? You'd marry the chauffeur and we'd all come to tea?*

~ SEASON 2, EPISODE 4

Set a rack on the bottom of a large pot with a lid and put the mold on the rack. Pour boiling water into the pot to reach halfway up the sides of the mold. Bring to a boil over high heat, reduce the heat to medium-low, cover, and slowly steam at a gentle boil for 2 hours. Check the water level every now and again and replenish with boiling water as needed to maintain the original level.

When the pudding is ready, carefully remove the mold from the pot and let stand for 15 minutes.

While the pudding rests, make the whipped cream and the syrup. In a bowl, using the electric mixer, beat the cream on medium speed until soft peaks form. Slowly add the granulated sugar while continuing to beat until stiff peaks form. Cover and refrigerate until serving.

For the syrup, in a small saucepan over high heat, bring the reserved fig liquid to a boil and boil until reduced to ½ cup (120 ml), about 5 minutes. Keep warm.

Uncover the mold, invert it onto a serving platter, and then tap the mold gently to release the pudding. To serve, cut into wedges and transfer to individual plates. Drizzle a little syrup alongside each wedge and top with the whipped cream.

BUTTERFLY CAKES

Posher British cousins of the traditional American cupcake, these pretty petite cakes
are topped with a dollop of whipped cream, a spot of jam, and a charming set of
"wings" fashioned from the domed cake tops—a perfect small and delicate bite
for any teatime tray.

FOR THE CAKES

1⅔ cups (215 g) flour

1¼ teaspoons baking powder

½ teaspoon salt

½ cup (115 g) unsalted butter, at room temperature

¾ cup (150 g) granulated sugar

2 eggs, at room temperature

½ teaspoon pure vanilla extract

½ cup (120 ml) milk

FOR THE TOPPING

½ cup (120 ml) heavy cream

1 tablespoon confectioners' sugar, plus more for dusting (optional)

1 tablespoon strawberry or raspberry jam

MAKES 12 SMALL CAKES

To make the cakes, preheat the oven to 350°F (180°C). Line
12 standard muffin cups with paper liners.

In a small bowl, whisk together the flour, baking powder, and salt.
In a large bowl, using an electric mixer, beat the butter on medium
speed until smooth, about 1 minute. Add the granulated sugar,
increase the speed to medium-high, and beat until fluffy and lighter
in color, 2–3 minutes. Add the eggs, one at a time, beating well after
each addition and adding the vanilla with the final egg. On low speed,
add about half of the flour mixture and mix just until blended, then
add the milk and again mix until blended. Add the remaining flour
mixture and mix just until blended.

Divide the batter evenly among the prepared cups and spread evenly.
Bake until a toothpick inserted into the center of a cake or two
comes out clean, 17–19 minutes. Let cool in the pan on a wire rack
for 15 minutes. Lift the cakes from the pan and arrange, top side up,
on the rack. Let cool completely.

To make the topping, in a bowl, using a handheld mixer, beat
together the cream and confectioners' sugar on medium speed
until stiff peaks form, 2–3 minutes. Use right away or cover and
refrigerate up to 2 hours before serving.

Just before serving, using a serrated knife, cut off the domed top
from each cake and cut in half crosswise to form the "wings."
Spoon (or pipe with a plain tip) some of the whipped cream onto
the center of the cupcake. Put a small dollop (about ¼ teaspoon)
of the jam onto the center of the whipped cream. Gently push
2 "wings," cut side down and at a slight angle, into the cream,
positioning them on either side of the jam. Lightly dust the top of
each cake with confectioners' sugar, if desired.

ROSE & VANILLA FAIRY CAKES

Fairy cakes are a British teatime classic and a favorite of children. Similar to modern cupcakes though smaller, the delicate cakes are traditionally bite-size sponge cakes dressed up with whimsical decorations. Nowadays, most fairy cakes are cupcake size and are often a butter cake rather than a sponge cake. Embellish these petite pink-frosted treats with pistachios and confectioners' sugar as suggested, or decorate them with sparkling sugar, frosting flowers, rose petals, or other edible blossoms.

FOR THE CAKES

1½ cups (185 g) self-rising flour

Pinch of kosher salt

¾ cup (170 g) unsalted butter

¾ cup (150 g) granulated sugar

1 tablespoon rose water

1½ teaspoons pure vanilla extract

3 eggs

FOR THE FROSTING

½ cup (115 g) unsalted butter, at cool room temperature

3 cups (340 g) confectioners' sugar, sifted

Pinch of kosher salt

1 tablespoon rose water

1 teaspoon pure vanilla extract

3 drops pink food coloring

2 tablespoons finely chopped pistachios (optional)

Confectioners' sugar, for dusting (optional)

MAKES 12 SMALL CAKES

To make the cakes, preheat the oven to 350°F (180°C). Line 12 standard muffin cups with paper liners.

Sift together the flour and salt into a small bowl. In a large bowl, using an electric mixer, beat together the butter and granulated sugar on medium-high speed until light and fluffy, about 3 minutes. Beat in the rose water and vanilla until blended. On medium speed, add the eggs, one at a time, beating well after each addition. On low speed, gradually add the flour mixture, mixing just until incorporated.

Spoon the batter into the prepared muffin cups, dividing it evenly. Bake until golden and a toothpick inserted into the center of a cake or two comes out clean, 15–20 minutes. Let cool completely in the pan on a wire rack, then remove from the pan.

To make the frosting, in a bowl, using the electric mixer, beat together the butter, confectioners' sugar, and salt on medium speed until smooth and fluffy, 2–3 minutes. Add the rose water, vanilla, and food coloring and beat until evenly colored.

Fit a piping bag with a small star tip, spoon the frosting into the bag, and secure closed. Pipe the frosting onto the top of each cupcake. Sprinkle with the pistachios and dust with confectioners' sugar (if using) and serve.

APPLE CRUMBLE CAKE

There were numerous apple varieties available in Edwardian England, and
the fruit was extremely popular for use in both cooking and baking. When
you can, select heirloom varieties, which are both tarter and more versatile.
Granny Smith and Cox's Orange Pippin are good choices, as is the Braeburn.
Bramley is the best-known cooking variety in Britain and a sound
bet for any baking recipe.

FOR THE CAKE

Unsalted butter, for the pan

**3 cups (375 g) flour, plus
more for the pan**

1 teaspoon baking soda

1 teaspoon ground cinnamon

¼ teaspoon salt

1 cup (200 g) granulated sugar

**1 cup (210 g) firmly packed
light brown sugar**

¾ cup (180 ml) canola oil

**¾ cup (170 g) unsweetened
applesauce**

3 eggs

**3 baking apples, peeled,
cored, and cut into cubes**

FOR THE TOPPING

1 cup (125 g) flour

**½ cup (115 g) cold unsalted
butter, cut into cubes**

**½ cup (100 g) firmly
packed light brown sugar**

SERVES 12

To make the cake, preheat the oven to 350°F (180°C). Lightly butter
a 9 x 13-inch (23 x 33-cm) baking pan, then dust with flour, tapping
out the excess.

In a large bowl, stir together the flour, baking soda, cinnamon,
and salt. In a medium bowl, whisk together both sugars, the oil,
applesauce, and eggs until blended. Make a well in the center of the
flour mixture, add the sugar mixture to the well, and stir just until
smooth. Add the apples and stir until evenly distributed. Spread the
batter in the prepared pan, smoothing the top.

To make the topping, in a bowl, combine the flour, butter, and
brown sugar. Using your fingers, work the ingredients together just
until evenly mixed. Press the mixture together into a ball and then
separate with your fingers into coarse crumbs. Sprinkle the crumbs
evenly over the top of the cake.

Bake the cake until a toothpick inserted into the center comes out
clean, about 1 hour. Let cool completely in the pan on a wire rack.
Cut into squares and serve.

RECIPE NOTE

If using a glass baking dish, lower the oven temperature to 325°F (165°C).

DUNDEE CAKE

Rumor has it that Mary, Queen of Scots, did not like candied cherries in her cakes, and the inception of this cake was the result of a workaround that swapped in blanched almonds for the customary stone fruit. James Keiller & Sons, a marmalade company in Dundee, Scotland, coined the name Dundee cake to describe the modern version, which it developed and began mass-producing in the mid-nineteenth century.

1 lb (450 g) mixed golden and dark raisins

6 tablespoons (90 ml) Scotch whisky

1 cup (225 g) butter, at room temperature, plus more for the pan

1 cup (210 g) firmly packed Demerara sugar

Pinch of salt

4 eggs

2¼ cups (280 g) flour

¼ teaspoon ground cinnamon

¼ teaspoon ground nutmeg

1 cup plus 2 tablespoons (115 g) ground almonds

½ cup (160 g) orange marmalade

Grated zest of 2 oranges

⅔ cup (95 g) whole blanched almonds, for decorating

SERVES 8–10

In a saucepan over low heat, combine the raisins and whisky and heat, stirring once or twice, until hot, 10–15 minutes. Remove from the heat and let steep for 2 hours.

Preheat the oven to 325°F (165°C). Butter the bottom and sides of a 9-inch (23-cm) round cake pan. Line the bottom with parchment paper and butter the parchment.

In a large bowl, using an electric mixer, beat the butter on medium speed until smooth, about 1 minute. Increase the speed to medium-high, add the sugar and salt, and beat until fluffy and lighter in color, 2–3 minutes. Add the eggs, one at a time, together with a spoonful of the flour with the first egg to stop the mix from curdling, beating well after each addition. Beat in the remaining flour and the cinnamon and nutmeg until incorporated. Using a wooden spoon, stir in the raisins and whisky, the ground almonds, marmalade, and orange zest until evenly distributed.

Transfer the batter to the prepared pan, spread evenly, and smooth the top. Arrange the whole blanched almonds on top in concentric circles, with the pointed end of each nut directed toward the center. Bake the cake until a toothpick inserted into the center comes out clean, 1½–1¾ hours. Let cool completely in the pan on a wire rack, then invert the pan onto the rack, lift off the pan, and peel off the parchment. Transfer the cake right side up to a serving plate and serve.

PARKIN

Warm spices, treacle, and oats form the basis of the beloved parkin cake, a gingerbread-like treat commonly eaten during the winter months. The amount of black treacle and golden syrup added varies from county to county, but the sticky, chewy, slightly nubby texture stays the same. In the United States, these two products can be found in well-stocked markets or online. Lyle's (Tate & Lyle) makes quality versions of both. If black treacle is not available, blackstrap molasses can be substituted in the same amount. Likewise, medium oats (not rolled oats) can be purchased online, or steel cut oats can be processed into a coarse meal and used as a substitute, as is done here.

½ cup (115 g) unsalted butter, plus more for the pan

1¼ cups (160 g) flour, plus more for the pan

¾ cup (150 g) firmly packed dark brown sugar

½ cup (170 g) black treacle or blackstrap molasses

½ cup (170 g) golden syrup

3 tablespoons milk

1 cup (175 g) steel cut oats

2 teaspoons baking powder

2 teaspoons ground ginger

1½ teaspoons mixed spice or pumpkin pie spice

¼ teaspoon salt

1 egg

SERVES 12

Preheat the oven to 300°F (150°C). Lightly butter the bottom and sides of an 8-inch (20-cm) square pan. Line the bottom with parchment paper, lightly butter the parchment, and then dust the bottom and sides with flour, tapping out the excess.

In a saucepan over medium heat, combine the butter, brown sugar, treacle, golden syrup, and milk and cook, stirring, until the butter and sugar are melted and the mixture is smooth, 4–6 minutes. Remove the pan from the heat and let cool for 5 minutes.

In a food processor, pulse the oats until they are coarsely chopped (there will be some finely ground and some coarse pieces), 1–2 minutes. Transfer to a bowl, add the flour, baking powder, ginger, mixed spice, and salt, and whisk until blended. Scrape the molasses mixture into the oat-flour mixture, add the egg, and stir until well blended.

Scrape the batter into the prepared pan and spread evenly. Bake until a toothpick inserted into the center of the cake comes out with only a few moist crumbs clinging to it, 75–80 minutes. The center will be slightly lower than the edges. Let cool in the pan on a wire rack for 20 minutes, then turn the cake out of the pan, peel off the parchment, turn right side up, and let cool completely.

Cut into small squares and store in an airtight container at room temperature for up to 1 week. The flavor and texture are best when the cake is made at least 3 days before serving.

SPICY DARK GINGERBREAD

Although the small English town of Market Drayton claims the title of Home
of Gingerbread, the spice-packed cake more likely entered Europe in the late
tenth century, thanks to an Armenian monk who settled in north-central
France, where he taught the locals how to make it. By the time gingerbread
found its way to Market Drayton, where it was first reportedly baked in the
early 1790s, treacle and flour had replaced the honey and bread crumbs of
the medieval formula and eggs and butter had found their way into the batter,
yielding a richer, lighter cake that later proved a perfect accompaniment to tea.

3 cups (375 g) flour

2 tablespoons ground ginger

1 teaspoon ground cinnamon

1 teaspoon ground allspice

1 teaspoon baking soda

½ teaspoon kosher salt

**¼ cup (35 g) peeled and
grated fresh ginger**

**1 cup (225 g) unsalted butter,
at room temperature**

**1 cup (225 g) firmly packed
light brown sugar**

1 egg

1 cup (340 g) light molasses

1 cup (240 ml) buttermilk

**Whipped cream, for
serving (optional)**

SERVES 10–12

Preheat the oven to 350°F (180°C). Butter two 8½ x 4½ x 2½-inch
(21.5 x 11.5 x 6-cm) loaf pans or a 10-inch (25-cm) Bundt pan, then
lightly dust with flour, tapping out the excess.

In a large bowl, whisk together the flour, ground ginger, cinnamon,
allspice, baking soda, salt, and fresh ginger. In another large bowl,
using an electric mixer, beat the butter on medium speed until
smooth, about 1 minute. Increase the speed to medium-high, add
the brown sugar, and beat until light and creamy, 2–3 minutes. Add
the egg and beat until incorporated, then add the molasses and beat
until well blended, about 2 minutes. On low speed, add the flour
mixture in three batches alternately with the buttermilk in two
batches, beginning and ending with the flour mixture and mixing well
after each addition. Transfer the batter to the prepared pan(s) and
smooth the surface.

Bake the cake until a toothpick inserted into the center comes
out clean, about 50 minutes. Let cool in the pan(s) on a wire rack
for 10 minutes. Run a thin-bladed knife around the inside of the
pan(s) to loosen any stuck edges, then turn the cake(s) out of the
pan(s) onto the rack. (If using loaf pans, turn the cakes right side up;
if using a Bundt pan, leave the cake inverted.) Let cool for at least
15 minutes before serving. Accompany each slice with whipped
cream, if you like.

BARA BRITH

The name of this Welsh teatime cakelike bread translates to "mottled bread" or "speckled bread," a nod to the copious amount of dried fruit in the loaf. The texture is moist and dense, and the sweetness is on the lighter side, with a touch of orange marmalade flavor. Here only currants are used, but a mixture of dried fruits—candied citrus peel, dark and golden raisins, cranberries—is common, with any larger pieces cut into bite-size bits. Soak the fruit in a strong black tea—Earl Grey or Irish breakfast is a good choice—for at least eight hours, so it absorbs as much of the tea as possible. This bread is delicious toasted and spread with butter.

1⅔ cups (240 g) dried currants

½ cup (120 ml) hot strong black tea

Unsalted butter, for the pan and for serving

1¾ cups (225 g) flour, plus more for the pan

⅔ cup (140 g) firmly packed dark brown sugar

2 teaspoons baking powder

1½ teaspoons mixed spice or pumpkin pie spice

¼ teaspoon salt

¼ cup (60 ml) water

1 egg, lightly whisked

2 tablespoons orange marmalade

SERVES 8–12

In a bowl, combine the currants and hot tea. Let stand, stirring occasionally, until the fruit is softened and the liquid is almost absorbed, 8–12 hours.

Preheat the oven to 325°F (165°C). Lightly butter an 8½ x 4½ x 2½-inch (21.5 x 11.5 x 6-cm) loaf pan, then dust with flour, tapping out the excess.

In a bowl, whisk together the flour, brown sugar, baking powder, mixed spice, and salt. Add the currants and any remaining soaking liquid, the water, egg, and marmalade and stir until well blended.

Transfer the batter to the prepared pan and spread evenly. Bake until a toothpick inserted into the center of the cake comes out clean, 72–75 minutes. Let cool in the pan on a wire rack for 20 minutes, then turn out onto the rack, turn right side up, and let cool completely.

To serve, cut into thick slices and serve at room temperature or toasted with butter.

HAZELNUT DACQUOISE

The term *dacquoise* refers to both the baked layers of nut meringue and the cake itself—yet another British import from the kitchens of French pastry chefs in the nineteenth century. Here, a single large *dacquoise* is made, suitable for cutting into narrow wedges for teatime. But the same ingredients can be fashioned into small meringues, which can be layered with the buttercream and served as bite-size treats.

FOR THE DACQUOISE

Unsalted butter and flour, for the pans

1⅓ cups (185 g) plus ¼ cup (35 g) hazelnuts, skinned and toasted

1 cup (200 g) granulated sugar

3 tablespoons Dutch-process cocoa powder

2 tablespoons cornstarch

6 egg whites, at room temperature

1 teaspoon pure vanilla extract

FOR THE BUTTERCREAM

2 cups (450 g) unsalted butter, at room temperature

3 cups (340 g) confectioners' sugar

1 teaspoon pure vanilla extract

1 teaspoon hazelnut extract

⅛ teaspoon kosher salt

Confectioners' sugar, for dusting

SERVES 8–10

To make the dacquoise, preheat the oven to 300°F (150°C). Lightly butter the bottom and sides of two 11 x 17-inch (28 x 43-cm) sheet pans. Cut a sheet of parchment paper to fit the bottom of each pan. Using an 8-inch (20-cm) round cake pan as a guide, trace two circles on each parchment sheet. Place each sheet, circles side down, on a prepared pan. Butter the paper, then flour the bottom and sides of the pan, tapping out the excess. You should be able to see the traced circles through the paper.

In a food processor or blender, combine 1⅓ cups (185 g) of the hazelnuts, ½ cup (100 g) of the granulated sugar, the cocoa powder, and the cornstarch and process until the nuts are ground to a powder.

In a large bowl, using an electric mixer, beat the egg whites on medium-high speed until they form soft peaks and have tripled in volume. With the mixer still on medium-high speed, slowly pour in the remaining ½ cup (100 g) granulated sugar and the vanilla and beat until the whites are stiff and glossy. Be careful not to overwhip the whites, or they will be dry and powdery.

Pour the hazelnut-sugar mixture over the beaten egg whites. Using a rubber spatula, fold in the nut mixture gently and quickly, with as few strokes as possible. Fit a piping bag with a ½-inch (12-mm) plain tip, spoon some of the batter into it, and secure closed.

Holding the bag upright just above a prepared pan and starting in the middle of a circle, pipe spirals of the batter until you reach the edge of the circle, covering the circle completely. Repeat to cover the second circle on the pan. Refill the bag as necessary and pipe the batter onto the circles on the second pan the same way, piping the fourth circle as full as possible with the batter you have left.

For a chocolate-hazelnut variation, substitute ganache for the buttercream. Combine 12 oz (340 g) finely chopped bittersweet or semisweet chocolate with 4 tablespoons (60 g) unsalted butter in a heatproof bowl. In a saucepan over medium-high heat, bring 1 cup (240 ml) heavy cream just to a boil. Remove from the heat and pour over the chocolate and butter. Stir with a wire whisk until smooth. Let cool until spreadable.

Bake the layers until they are crisp, dry, and beginning to brown, 50–60 minutes. They will feel crisp on top when done, but they might give a little while they are still warm. Let cool completely on the pans on wire racks. The layers will become crisp as they cool.

To make the buttercream, in a bowl, using the electric mixer on medium speed, beat the butter until smooth, about 2 minutes. Add the confectioners' sugar, vanilla and hazelnut extracts, and salt, increase the speed to medium-high, and beat until combined, stopping the mixer to scrape down the sides of the bowl as needed. Cover and refrigerate.

To assemble the cake, gently peel the cooled layers away from the parchment paper. Using a serrated knife and a sawing motion, trim the 3 solid layers so they are exactly the same size. Using a rolling pin, crush any trimmings along with the fourth round and transfer to a bowl. Finely chop the remaining ¼ cup (35 g) hazelnuts and add to the crushed trimmings. Set aside.

Place 1 layer on a large platter. Using an icing spatula, spread about ⅓ cup (80 g) buttercream in a thin, even layer on top. Place a second layer on top of the buttercream and spread with the same amount of buttercream. Place the third layer on top. Using as much of the remaining buttercream as needed, spread the top and sides of the cake with a thin coating, smoothing it as evenly as possible.

Coat the entire cake with the crumb-nut mixture, gently pressing it against the sides and top with your hands. Using a fine-mesh sieve, sift a light dusting of confectioners' sugar over the top. If desired, fit a clean piping bag with a small star tip, spoon any remaining buttercream into it, secure closed, and pipe a border of rosettes on the top of the cake. Slip a wide metal spatula underneath the cake and transfer it to a serving plate.

The cake can be cut right away, but it is easier to cut if it is first allowed to soften for several hours in the refrigerator. It will keep, well covered in the refrigerator, for up to 2 days. Slice into wedges with a sharp chef's knife or a serrated knife and serve at room temperature.

ALMOND CAKE

Almonds have been imported by the British since medieval times and have long been a common addition to cake recipes. Here, ground almonds and almond extract impart a bold flavor to this rich, moist, nutty teatime favorite. In late spring, when cherries are in season, add them to the table to echo the kirsch in the hot syrup used to infuse the warm cake.

FOR THE CAKE

Unsalted butter, for the pan

1 cup (100 g) ground almonds

½ cup (60 g) flour

1 teaspoon baking powder

1¼ cups (250 g) granulated sugar

6 eggs, separated, at room temperature

Grated zest of 1 lemon

1 teaspoon pure almond extract

FOR THE SYRUP

3 tablespoons kirsch

1 tablespoon fresh lemon juice

2 tablespoons granulated sugar

Confectioners' sugar, for dusting

SERVES 8–10

Preheat the oven to 325°F (165°C). Butter the bottom and sides of a 9-inch (23-cm) springform pan and line the bottom with parchment paper.

To make the cake, in a medium bowl, whisk together the ground almonds, flour, and baking powder. In a large bowl, using an electric mixer, beat together the sugar, egg yolks, and lemon zest on medium speed until thick and pale, about 10 minutes. Add the ground almond mixture and almond extract and stir with a wooden spoon to blend well.

In a bowl, using clean beaters, beat the egg whites on medium-high speed until soft peaks form. Using a rubber spatula, fold the beaten whites into the egg yolk mixture just until no white streaks remain.

Pour the batter into the prepared pan and gently smooth the top. Bake the cake until the top springs back when lightly touched, about 1 hour. Transfer the pan to a wire rack and remove the pan sides.

To make the syrup, in a small saucepan over medium heat, combine the kirsch, lemon juice, and granulated sugar and heat, stirring, until the sugar dissolves and the mixture is hot. Remove from the heat and brush the hot syrup gently and evenly over the hot cake. Let the cake cool completely.

Just before serving, lightly dust the top of the cake with confectioners' sugar.

WALNUT TORTE

In the 1870s, afternoon tea at home was enjoyed by both the rich and the poor, with the lower classes especially keen to take up a custom that was enjoyed by the gentry. By the Edwardian period, tearooms were popping up everywhere, and afternoon tea was no longer something done only at home. The sweets at these new outposts varied according to how fancy the surroundings were. This classic nut torte would not have been out of place in the finest tearooms.

1¾ cups (200 g) walnut or pecan pieces

2 tablespoons flour

¼ teaspoon salt

6 eggs, separated, at room temperature

⅔ cup (140 g) sugar

SERVES 10–12

Preheat the oven to 325°F (165°C). Line the bottom of a 9-inch (23-cm) round cake pan with parchment paper.

In a food processor, combine the walnuts, flour, and salt and process until the nuts are finely ground; do not overprocess.

In a large bowl, using an electric mixer, beat together the egg yolks and ⅓ cup (70 g) of the sugar on medium-high speed until pale and thick, 3–5 minutes. Using a rubber spatula, fold the walnut mixture into the egg yolk mixture just until evenly mixed.

In a large bowl, using clean beaters, beat the egg whites on medium speed until they start to foam. Add about one-third of the remaining sugar and beat until the whites are opaque. Add about half of the remaining sugar and continue to beat until the whites start to increase in volume and become firm. Add the remaining sugar, increase the speed to high, and beat until the whites form soft peaks but still look wet. Using the spatula, fold one-third of the whites into the walnut mixture, then gently fold in the remaining whites just until no white streaks remain.

Transfer the batter to the prepared pan and smooth the top. Bake the torte until lightly browned and a toothpick inserted into the center comes out clean, 35–40 minutes. Let cool completely in the pan on a wire rack.

Run a thin-bladed knife around the inside of the pan to loosen the torte sides, then invert the pan onto a serving plate, lift off the pan, and peel off the parchment. Turn the torte right side up on the plate and cut into wedges to serve.

PLUM BUTTER CAKE

With the invention of modern baking powder in England in 1843, a wealth of new baking opportunities suddenly became possible. Even the traditional English pound cake, made with equal parts butter, flour, sugar, and eggs, was given a shot of the modern leavener, resulting in the lighter, fluffier butter cake. For this rich teatime offering, the Downton kitchen would have turned to the Victoria, Farleigh damson, or another good cooking plum, perhaps from the estate's own garden.

1 cup (225 g) unsalted butter, at room temperature, plus more for the pan

1½ cups (185 g) flour

1 teaspoon baking powder

¼ teaspoon salt

¾ cup (150 g) plus 1 tablespoon sugar

2 eggs

6–8 plums, about 1 lb (450 g), pitted and thickly sliced

¼ teaspoon ground cinnamon

SERVES 6

Position a rack in the lower third of the oven and preheat the oven to 350°F (180°C). Butter a 9-inch (23-cm) round or 8-inch (20-cm) square cake pan. Line the bottom with parchment paper and butter the parchment.

Sift together the flour, baking powder, and salt into a bowl. In another bowl, using an electric mixer, beat the butter on medium speed until smooth, about 1 minute. Increase the speed to medium-high, add ¾ cup (150 g) of the sugar, and beat until fluffy and lighter in color, 2–3 minutes. Add the eggs, one at a time, beating well after each addition. On low speed, add the flour mixture and mix just until blended.

Transfer the batter to the prepared pan, spread evenly, and smooth the top. Poke the plum slices into the batter, placing them close together and covering the top completely. In a small bowl, stir together the cinnamon and the remaining 1 tablespoon sugar and sprinkle evenly over the plums.

Bake the cake until the top is golden, the edges pull away from the pan, and a toothpick inserted into the center comes out clean, 50–60 minutes. Let cool in the pan on a wire rack for about 30 minutes before serving. Serve warm.

LEMON DRIZZLE CAKE

Warne's Model Cookery and Housekeeping Book, published in 1868 in both London and New York, contains one of the earliest recipes for lemon cake, which calls for just four ingredients: eggs, flour, sugar, and grated lemon peel. A staple of tearooms in the National Trust properties and regularly voted among the top ten favorite cakes in Britain, this deliciously sticky, moist version is slightly more elaborate yet just as traditional.

FOR THE CAKE

½ cup (115 g) unsalted butter, at room temperature, plus more for the pan

1½ cups (185 g) flour, plus more for the pan

1 teaspoon baking powder

½ teaspoon salt

¾ cup (150 g) granulated sugar

1 tablespoon grated lemon zest

3 eggs

½ cup (120 ml) milk

1 teaspoon pure vanilla extract

FOR THE SYRUP

3 tablespoons fresh lemon juice

3 tablespoons granulated sugar

FOR THE GLAZE

½ cup (60 g) confectioners' sugar

1 tablespoon fresh lemon juice

SERVES 8

To make the cake, preheat the oven to 375°F (190°C). Butter a 9 x 5 x 3-inch (23 x 13 x 7.5-cm) loaf pan, then dust with flour, tapping out the excess.

Sift together the flour, baking powder, and salt into a bowl. In a large bowl, using an electric mixer, beat together the butter, granulated sugar, and lemon zest on medium-high speed until fluffy and lighter in color, about 3 minutes. Add the eggs, one at a time, beating well after each addition. Add the milk and vanilla and beat until blended. On low speed, add the flour mixture and beat just until blended.

Transfer the batter to the prepared pan and smooth the surface. Bake the cake until golden brown and a toothpick inserted into the center comes out clean, about 55 minutes. Let the cake cool in the pan on a wire rack for a few minutes, then turn it out onto the rack. Turn the cake on its side to cool while you make the syrup.

To make the syrup, in a small saucepan over medium heat, combine the lemon juice and granulated sugar. Bring to a simmer, stirring to dissolve the sugar, and then simmer until syrupy, about 2 minutes. Remove from the heat.

Using a long wooden skewer, pierce the sides and the bottom of the warm cake, making the holes about 1 inch (2.5 cm) apart and 1 inch (2.5 cm) deep. Brush the sides and bottom of the cake generously with the syrup, making sure it seeps into the holes.

To make the glaze, in a small bowl, whisk together the confectioners' sugar and lemon juice until smooth. When the cake is cool, turn it right side up on a serving plate and drizzle the glaze over the top. Let stand until the glaze is set, about 15 minutes, and serve.

ECCLES CAKES

The first official Eccles cakes were sold in 1793 from a bakery in the town of Eccles, in Lancashire. The light, flaky pastry for these small currant-filled sweets is a cross between a pie dough and a puff pastry dough, with just a hint of sweetness. It's said that these gems are typically 40 percent filling and 60 percent pastry, to ensure the perfect balance of sweet fruit and crispy, buttery pastry.

FOR THE PASTRY

2 cups (250 g) flour, plus more for the work surface and rolling

2 tablespoons granulated sugar

½ teaspoon salt

1 cup (225 g) cold unsalted butter, diced

⅓ cup (80 ml) ice-cold water

FOR THE FILLING

2 tablespoons firmly packed light brown sugar

2 tablespoons unsalted butter, at very soft room temperature

1 teaspoon mixed spice or pumpkin pie spice

¼ teaspoon grated lemon zest

¼ teaspoon grated orange zest

⅔ cup (95 g) dried currants

¼ cup (35 g) chopped mixed candied orange and lemon peel

1 tablespoon brandy or Cognac (optional)

FOR ASSEMBLY

1 egg white, lightly whisked

Demerara sugar, for sprinkling (optional)

MAKES 16 CAKES

To make the pastry, in a food processor, combine the flour, sugar, and salt and process until blended, about 5 seconds. Scatter the butter over the flour mixture and process until the butter is coated and slightly chopped, about 2 seconds. Sprinkle the water over the flour and butter and process until the dough comes together in small, moist crumbs, 7–10 seconds.

Scrape the dough onto a lightly floured work surface and shape into a rough rectangle. Roll out into a 6 x 18-inch (15 x 45-cm) rectangle, lightly flouring the dough and work surface as needed. The edges will be ragged. Fold the short ends toward each other so they meet in the middle. Fold the dough crosswise in half to make a 4½ x 6-inch (11.5 x 15-cm) rectangle. Rotate the dough so the seam is on the right and repeat the rolling and folding technique. Divide the dough crosswise into 2 equal rectangles (about 10½ oz/300 g) each. Wrap the rectangles in storage wrap and refrigerate until well chilled, about 2 hours or up to overnight.

To make the filling, in a bowl, combine the brown sugar, butter, mixed spice, and lemon and orange zest and, using a rubber spatula, mix until well blended. Add the currants, candied peel, and brandy (if using) and stir until well blended. Divide the mixture into 16 small mounds (about 2 teaspoons each), arrange on a plate, and flatten slightly (about 1½ inches/4 cm in diameter). Cover and refrigerate for at least 20 minutes or up to overnight.

Recipe continues on the following page

MOLESLEY: *It's hard to cope with three ladies at once.*
What with the tweeds and evening dresses and tea gowns, an' all.

MRS. HUGHES: *Tea gowns? We're not in the 1890s now, Mr. Molesley.*

CARSON: *More's the pity.*

~ SEASON 5, EPISODE 9

Continued

Preheat the oven to 400°F (200°C). Line a sheet pan with parchment paper.

To assemble the cakes, place half of the pastry dough on a lightly floured work surface and roll out ³⁄₁₆ inch (5 mm) thick. Using a 4-inch (10-cm) round cutter, cut out as many rounds from the dough as possible. If needed, gather together the dough scraps, press together, reroll, and cut out more rounds until you have a total of 8 rounds. Cover the rounds with plastic wrap and repeat with the remaining dough.

Working with 1 round at a time, arrange 1 mound of the filling in the center of the round and brush a little water around the edges of the pastry. Pleat the edges into the middle, covering the filling, and squeeze the edges together gently to seal. Place the pastry, seam side down, on a prepared sheet pan and flatten to form an oval about 2½ inches (6 cm) in diameter. Some of the fruit will be visible through the dough; try not to let it poke through the surface. Brush with a little of the egg white, sprinkle with the Demerara sugar (if using), and cut three slits in the top. Repeat with the remaining dough rounds and filling, arranging the cakes about 1½ inches (4 cm) apart on the prepared pan.

Bake the cakes until they are deep golden brown, 22–25 minutes. Let cool on the pan on a wire rack for at least 10 minutes before serving. Serve warm or at room temperature. The cakes are best when served the same day. They can be reheated in a preheated 300°F (150°C) oven, if desired.

YORKSHIRE TARTS

Traditionally, the custard filling in these tarts was made from curds left over from cheese making. If you are making the creamy curds from scratch, begin a day or two in advance to allow time for them to drain. A specialty of Yorkshire, where *Downton Abbey* is set, these tarts are a shining addition to a teatime table.

FOR THE FILLING

1½ cups (385 g) Homemade Curd Cheese (facing page) or store-bought whole-milk ricotta cheese or cottage cheese

4 tablespoons (60 g) unsalted butter, at room temperature

⅓ cup (70 g) sugar

1 whole egg

1 egg yolk

¾ teaspoon grated lemon zest

¼ cup (35 g) dried currants

Pinch of ground nutmeg

FOR THE PASTRY

1 cup (125 g) flour

3 tablespoons confectioners' sugar

¼ teaspoon salt

6 tablespoons (90 g) cold unsalted butter, cut into 8 pieces, plus room-temperature butter for the muffin cups

1 egg yolk, lightly whisked

MAKES 10 TARTS

To begin making the filling, prepare the curd cheese as directed. If using store-bought ricotta or cottage cheese, place a fine-mesh sieve over a bowl and spoon the cheese into the sieve. Cover and refrigerate to drain for at least 8 hours or up to overnight.

To make the pastry, in a food processor, combine the flour, confectioners' sugar, and salt and process until blended, about 5 seconds. Scatter the butter pieces over the flour mixture and pulse until the flour mixture forms coarse crumbs, 1–2 minutes. Drizzle the egg over the flour mixture and pulse just until the dough forms moist crumbs, about 10 seconds. Pour the crumbs onto a sheet of plastic wrap, cover with the wrap, and shape into a disk. Refrigerate for at least 30 minutes or up to overnight.

Lightly butter the bottom and sides of 10 standard muffin cups and line the bottom of each cup with parchment paper. Divide the dough into 10 equal pieces (1 slightly rounded tablespoon/20 g each) and roll each piece into a ball. Working with 1 ball at a time and using a lightly floured thumb, gently press the dough onto the bottom and up the sides of a prepared cup, stopping to within ⅛ inch (3 mm) of the rim. Repeat with the remaining dough balls. Cover the pan and refrigerate for at least 20 minutes or up to overnight.

Position a rack in the lower third of the oven and preheat the oven to 375°F (190°C).

To make the filling, in a bowl, using an electric mixer, beat together the drained cheese, butter, and sugar on medium speed until well blended and smooth, 2–3 minutes. Add the whole egg, egg yolk, and lemon zest and beat until just blended, 30–60 seconds. Using a wooden spoon, stir in the currants until evenly distributed.

HOMEMADE CURD CHEESE

6 cups (1.4 l) milk

¼ teaspoon salt

3 tablespoons fresh lemon juice

RECIPE NOTE

The recipe for homemade curd cheese yields about 1¾ cups (450 g). If pressed for time, use store-bought whole-milk ricotta cheese or cottage cheese; it will still need to be drained for at least 8 hours.

Spoon the custard into the tart shells, dividing it evenly (about ¼ cup/60 g each). Top each tart with a touch of nutmeg. Bake the tarts until the filling is puffed and jiggles slightly when the pan is nudged and the crust is golden brown, 21–23 minutes. Let cool completely in the pan on a wire rack. Run a thin-bladed knife between the tart and the cup to loosen each tart, then cover the pan and refrigerate until chilled, 1–2 hours.

To serve, carefully invert the muffin pan onto a large cutting board, releasing the tarts. Transfer the tarts, custard side up, to a large serving plate or individual plates.

To prepare the curd cheese, in a large stainless-steel pot, stir together the milk and salt. Place over medium heat and bring to a boil, stirring occasionally and regularly scraping down the sides and across the bottom of the pan to prevent scorching. When the milk is at a boil, slide the pot off the heat, add the lemon juice, and stir until the mixture begins to separate, about 1 minute. Let stand for 15 minutes.

Place a large fine-mesh sieve over a large bowl and line with a double layer of cheesecloth. Ladle the milk curds and liquid (whey) into the lined sieve. Set aside for 1–2 hours to drain, emptying the whey from the bowl as needed, until most of the liquid has drained out and the cheese is drier and firmer. Cover the bowl-and-sieve setup and refrigerate overnight. The next day, use the cheese immediately, or spoon into a container, cover, and refrigerate for up to 3 days.

RASPBERRY CUSTARD CAKE

Bursting with the flavor of fresh raspberries and vanilla custard, this simple one-layer cake boasts a moist and tender texture. It is perfect at teatime, of course, but it is also welcome as a finish to lunch or dinner.

FOR THE CUSTARD

3 egg yolks

3 tablespoons granulated sugar

Pinch of salt

¾ cup (180 ml) milk

¼ cup (60 ml) heavy cream

1 teaspoon pure vanilla extract or vanilla bean paste

FOR THE CAKE

¾ cup (170 g) unsalted butter, at room temperature, plus more for the pan

1¾ cups (220== g) flour, plus more for the pan

1½ teaspoons baking powder

½ teaspoon salt

1 cup (200 g) granulated sugar

3 eggs, at room temperature

1½ teaspoons pure vanilla extract

1½ cups (170 g) raspberries

2 tablespoons sliced almonds, toasted

Confectioners' sugar, for dusting

SERVES 8–12

To make the custard, in a saucepan, whisk together the egg yolks, granulated sugar, and salt until blended and lighter in color, about 1 minute. Pour in the milk and cream and whisk until blended, about 30 seconds. Place over medium-low heat and cook, stirring constantly, until the mixture is thick enough to coat the back of a spoon and hold a line drawn through it with your finger, 4–5 minutes. (It should register 170°F/77°C on an instant-read thermometer.) Remove from the heat, add the vanilla, and whisk until blended. Scrape into a small bowl and let cool to room temperature, then cover and refrigerate until cold, 2–3 hours or up to 2 days. For faster cooling, set the bowl over a larger bowl filled with ice and water and stir until cold. You should have 1¼ cups (310 g).

To make the cake, preheat the oven to 350°F (180°C). Lightly butter the bottom and sides of a 10-inch (25-cm) square cake pan or a 10-inch (25-cm) round springform pan, then dust with flour, tapping out the excess.

Have the cold custard ready. In a small bowl, whisk together the flour, baking powder, and salt. In a large bowl, using an electric mixer, beat the butter on medium speed until smooth, about 1 minute. Increase the speed to medium-high, add the sugar, and beat until fluffy and lighter in color, 2–3 minutes. Add the eggs, one at a time, beating well after each addition and adding the vanilla with the final egg. On low speed, add half the flour mixture and mix just until blended, then add half of the custard and mix just until blended. Add the remaining flour mixture and again mix just until blended.

Transfer the batter to the prepared pan, spread evenly, and smooth the top. Scatter the berries over the batter, drizzle the remaining custard on top, and finish with the sliced almonds. Bake the cake until a toothpick inserted into the center comes out clean, 43–45 minutes. Let cool in the pan on a wire rack for at least 20 minutes. Serve warm.

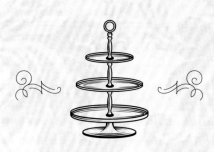

TEA SANDWICHES
& SAVORY BITES

MINI PORK PIES

Traditionally made with a heavy lard-infused dough, these savory mini pies instead use a butter-and-shortening crust. The result is a lighter, flakier, and more flavorful pastry. The quail egg is optional but a fun addition. If you're not using the egg, the pies will be slightly less full. Either way, Mrs. Patmore would surely approve.

FOR THE PASTRY

2½ cups (320 g) flour, plus more for the work surface

¾ teaspoon salt

½ cup (115 g) cold unsalted butter, diced

¼ cup (60 g) cold solid vegetable shortening, diced

⅓ cup (80 ml) very cold water

2 teaspoons fresh lemon juice

FOR THE FILLING

8 quail eggs (optional)

1 lb (450 g) ground pork

6 slices bacon (4 oz/115 g), chopped

3 tablespoons finely diced yellow onion

1 teaspoon salt

½ teaspoon dried thyme or sage (optional)

Good pinch of ground nutmeg (optional)

Good pinch of black pepper

FOR ASSEMBLY

Unsalted butter, for the muffin cups

2 teaspoons unseasoned fine dried bread crumbs

1 egg, lightly whisked

MAKES 8 PIES

To make the pastry, in a food processor, combine the flour and salt and process until blended, about 5 seconds. Scatter the butter and shortening over the flour mixture and process briefly until the butter is coated with flour and slightly chopped, about 2 seconds. Sprinkle the water and lemon juice over the flour mixture and process until the dough comes together in small, moist crumbs, 7–10 seconds.

Scrape the dough onto a lightly floured work surface and shape into a thick rectangle, then divide into 2 pieces, one twice as large as the other. Wrap in storage wrap and refrigerate until well chilled, about 2 hours or up to overnight. You should have about 1¼ lb (570 g) dough.

To make the filling, if using the quail eggs, fill a saucepan three-fourths full with water and bring to a boil over high heat. Gently lower the eggs into the water and cook for 2 minutes. Using a slotted spoon, transfer the eggs to a bowl of ice water to stop the cooking. While the eggs are still warm, carefully peel away the shells. Set the eggs aside, or cover and refrigerate for 1 hour or up to overnight.

In a bowl, combine the pork, bacon, onion, salt, thyme (if using), nutmeg (if using), and pepper and mix until well blended. Set aside, or cover and refrigerate for 1 hour or up to overnight.

Line an 11 x 17-inch (28 x 43-cm) sheet pan with aluminum foil. Position a rack in the lower third of the oven, place the foil-lined pan on the rack, and preheat the oven to 425°F (220°C). Lightly butter the bottom and sides of 8 standard muffin cups, then line the bottoms with parchment paper.

To assemble the pies, on a lightly floured work surface, roll out the larger portion of pastry ⅛ inch (3 mm) thick. Cut out 8 rounds each 4¾ inches (12 cm) in diameter. If necessary, gather up the scraps, press together, reroll, and cut out more rounds to total 8 rounds.

RECIPE NOTE

Any chunky sausage, such as breakfast or a sweet Italian (use 1¼ lb/570 g), is a good substitute for the pork-bacon mixture.

Cover the rounds with storage wrap to prevent drying. On the lightly floured work surface, roll out the smaller portion of pastry ⅛ inch (3 mm) thick. Cut out 8 rounds each 3 inches (7.5 cm) in diameter, repeating the gathering and rerolling if necessary. Cut out a ½-inch (12-mm) round from the center of each 3-inch (7.5-cm) round. Cover the rounds to prevent drying.

Line the prepared muffin cups with the larger rounds, pressing each round into the bottom and up the sides. Scatter the bread crumbs in the pastry-lined cups, dividing the crumbs evenly. If using the quail eggs, spoon half of the pork mixture into the cups, dividing it evenly and pressing gently to fill the bottom and to make a shallow well in the center. Arrange a quail egg in each well and top with an equal amount of the remaining filling, doming the mixture slightly in the center. If not using the quail eggs, fill each cup with an equal amount of the meat mixture, doming the mixture slightly in the center. You'll use a total of about ⅓ cup (70 g) of the meat mixture in each cup. Brush the inside edges of the dough with some of the beaten egg. Top each cup with a smaller pastry round, pinch the bottom and top pastries together, and roll the pressed edges inward to seal completely. Brush the tops with more beaten egg.

Reduce the oven temperature to 400°F (200°C). Place the muffin pan on the prepared sheet pan and bake the pies until they are deep golden brown, 40–43 minutes. Transfer the sheet pan to a wire rack and let the pies cool for 10 minutes. Run a thin-bladed knife between each pie and the cup sides to loosen the pie from the pan, then remove the pies from the pan.

Serve the pies warm or at room temperature. The pies are best when served the same day they are baked. They can be reheated in a 300°F (150°C) oven, if desired.

GOUGÈRES

The small, light, and airy *gougère* of the afternoon tea tray is rooted in Burgundy, where it first appeared in the seventeenth century and continues to be the preferred accompaniment to wine tasting in the local cellars. These pastries grew in prominence in the nineteenth century, spreading beyond central France and taking on new flavorings. But traditional cooks kept their classic composition of alpine cheese (typically Gruyère, Comté, or Emmentaler) and rich butter-and-egg choux pastry—a formula that would be put to work in the Downton kitchen.

**2 cups (480 ml) plus
2 tablespoons milk**

½ cup (115 g) unsalted butter

2 teaspoons salt

2 cups (250 g) flour

8 eggs

**½ lb (225 g) Gruyère,
Emmentaler, or other
Swiss-type cheese,
finely shredded**

MAKES ABOUT 48 PUFFS

Preheat the oven to 375°F (190°C). Line two sheet pans with parchment paper.

In a heavy saucepan over high heat, combine 2 cups (480 ml) of the milk, the butter, and salt and bring to a boil. Add the flour all at once, reduce the heat to low, and stir until the mixture forms a ball and pulls cleanly away from the sides of the pan, about 5 minutes. Remove from the heat and let cool for 2 minutes.

Using an electric mixer on medium speed, add the eggs, one at a time, beating well after each addition until thoroughly incorporated and the dough is very shiny; this step should take about 5 minutes. Stir in three-fourths of the cheese.

Using a spoon, scoop out rounds 2–3 inches (5–7.5 cm) in diameter onto the prepared sheet pans, spacing them about 2 inches (5 cm) apart. Brush the rounds with the remaining 2 tablespoons milk, then sprinkle evenly with the remaining cheese.

Bake the pastries until well puffed and golden brown, 30–35 minutes. Let the pastries cool briefly on the pans on wire racks and serve warm, or let cool completely and serve at room temperature.

CHEESE BOUCHÉES

Bouchée, literally "mouthful," is a French pastry with a savory or sweet filling. According to legend, these rich, flaky pastries were created in the palace kitchen of Louis XV at the request of Queen Marie and made their way to the finest tables of neighboring Britain, as evidenced by Alfred's making a batch of them in season 4 of *Downton.* Bouchées vary in size, with the smaller ones suitable for serving as an *amuse-bouche,* an hors d'oeuvre, a canapé, or a tasty offering on the afternoon tea tray.

FOR THE PASTRY

1⅓ cups (165 g) flour, plus more for the work surface

6 tablespoons (90 g) cold salted butter, cut into small cubes

4–5 tablespoons (60–75 ml) ice-cold water

FOR THE FILLING

1 egg

¼ cup (30 g) grated sharp Cheddar cheese

¼ cup (30 g) grated Parmesan cheese

1 tablespoon salted butter, melted and cooled

Pinch of cayenne pepper (optional)

Salt and black pepper

Milk, for sealing and brushing

MAKES ABOUT
20 BOUCHÉES

To make the pastry, put the flour into a bowl, scatter the butter over the top, and work the butter into the flour with a pastry blender or your fingertips until the mixture is the consistency of bread crumbs. Add just enough of the water, stirring and tossing the flour mixture with a fork as you do, until the dough comes together in a rough mass. Shape into a ball, wrap in storage wrap, and refrigerate for 20–30 minutes.

To make the filling, in a bowl, whisk the egg until blended. Add both cheeses, the butter, cayenne (if using), and a little salt and black pepper and mix well.

Preheat the oven to 400°F (200°C). Line a sheet pan with parchment paper.

Divide the dough in half. Re-cover and refrigerate half. On a lightly floured work surface, roll out the other half into a round about ¹⁄₁₆ inch (2 mm) thick. Using a 3½-inch (9-cm) round cutter, cut out as many rounds as possible. To shape each pastry, put about ¾ teaspoon of the filling on half of a dough round, leaving the edge uncovered. Brush the entire edge of the round with milk, then fold

MRS. HUGHES: *I have a confession.*
I let them have their tea in my sitting room.

CARSON: *That was nice of you.*

MRS. HUGHES: *It was quite nice. But I had my reasons.*
There's a grating on the wall which means you can hear
what's being said in the room.

~ SEASON 2, EPISODE 1

the uncovered half over the filling to form a half-moon, pressing the edges to seal. Bring the corners together and press firmly, sealing them well (like shaping tortellini). Transfer the filled pastries to the prepared pan and refrigerate them while you roll out, fill, and shape the remaining dough.

Arrange all the filled pastries on the pan, spacing them about 1½ inches (4 cm) apart. Lightly brush the tops with milk. Bake the pastries until golden brown, 22–24 minutes. Let the pastries cool briefly on the pan on a wire rack and serve warm, or let cool completely and serve at room temperature.

CORNISH PASTIES

Few foods have a greater regional history than the pasty, a minced meat pie that dates from medieval times but became particularly common in the sixteenth century as a simple meal for tin miners in rural Cornwall. A miner could easily transport the pasty (usually filled with vegetables rather than more costly meat) to work, keep it warm in the mine, and eat it without utensils. If the pasty grew cold, the miner would place it on a shovel and warm it over a fire. The basic pasty recipe survived into the Edwardian era, where its appeal as an accompaniment to afternoon tea—depending on its size and on the refinement of its filling and its pastry—reached across the classes.

FOR THE PASTRY

4½ cups (560 g) all-purpose flour, plus more for the work surface

1¼ teaspoons salt

7½ oz (210 g) suet, solid vegetable shortening, or salted butter, shredded or cut into bits

1 cup plus 2 tablespoons (270 ml) cold water

MAKES 12 PASTIES

To make the pastry, in a large bowl, combine the flour, salt, and suet and quickly mix with your fingertips until the mixture resembles coarse crumbs. Using a pastry blender or a fork, mix in the water, a little at a time, until the mixture is evenly moistened and can be formed into a ball. Divide the dough in half and pat each half into a disk. Wrap each disk in plastic wrap and refrigerate while you make the filling.

To make the filling, in a bowl, combine the apples, pork, bacon, Worcestershire sauce, and sage and stir to mix well. Season with salt and pepper.

Preheat the oven to 375°F (190°C). Line a sheet pan with parchment paper.

On a generously floured work surface, roll out 1 dough disk about ⅛ inch (3 mm) thick. Using a saucer as a guide, cut out 6 circles each about 6 inches (15 cm) in diameter. (If needed, gather up the dough scraps, press together, reroll, and cut out more circles until you have 6 circles.) Divide half of the filling evenly among the circles,

FOR THE FILLING

2 small apples, such as Granny Smith or Cox's Orange Pippin, peeled, halved, cored, and cut into ½-inch (12-mm) cubes

7 oz (200 g) boneless pork shoulder, trimmed of excess fat and cut into ½-inch (12-mm) cubes

¼ lb (115 g) bacon, minced

1 tablespoon Worcestershire sauce

1 teaspoon dried sage, or 1 tablespoon minced fresh sage

Salt and black pepper

spooning it onto half of each circle and leaving ½ inch (12 mm) uncovered around the edge. With a fingertip, dampen the edge of each circle with water, fold the circles in half, and press down on the edge to seal. Crimp the edges with a fork or with your fingers then fold or roll the end corners underneath. Prick the tops several times with a fork to vent and arrange on the prepared sheet pan, spacing them well apart. Repeat with the remaining pastry and filling.

Bake the pasties until barely golden on top and a thermometer inserted into the center of a pasty registers 165°F (74°C), about 20 minutes. Transfer to a wire rack to cool. Serve warm or at room temperature.

ROBERT: *As usual our expectations are disappointed. Let's have some tea.*

~ SEASON 3, EPISODE 8

TEA SANDWICHES

With lunch at noon and dinner at eight, the afternoon tea proved the perfect answer to snacking politely before mealtime, and small, delicate finger sandwiches played a big role in quelling late-afternoon hunger. Custom dictated the sandwiches be made with two thin, crustless slices of bread. The filling was most commonly butter, mayonnaise, or cream cheese and paper-thin vegetable slices, or flavorful combinations like Cheddar cheese and pickle relish and ham and English mustard, though the offerings went beyond these classics.

CUCUMBER

¾ English cucumber

Salt

8 thin slices good-quality white bread, such as pain de mie

Unsalted butter, at room temperature

White pepper

SERVES 4–6

Slice the cucumber as thinly as possible. Put the slices into a colander in the sink or into a sieve over a bowl, sprinkle lightly with salt, and let stand for 20 minutes. Taste a slice to make sure you haven't added too much salt. If you discover you have, rinse the slices briefly under cool running water. Lay a few paper towels on a work surface, arrange the cucumber slices in a single layer on the towels, and pat the slices dry.

Lay the bread slices on a work surface and spread each slice generously with butter. Arrange the cucumber slices, overlapping them, on 4 of the bread slices and sprinkle with pepper. Top with the remaining bread slices, buttered side down.

Using a serrated knife, cut off the crusts from each sandwich, then cut the sandwiches into neat fingers, triangles, or quarters.

Recipe continues on the following page

TEA ETIQUETTE

Today, triangle-shaped sandwiches are fashionable, but in the Edwardian era, sandwiches were commonly rectangular. The crusts should always be trimmed off, then the sandwiches cut into the desired shape and neatly stacked.

Continued

DEVILED EGG & CRESS

4 eggs

4 tablespoons (60 g) unsalted butter, at room temperature

¼ cup (60 ml) mayonnaise

1 teaspoon finely chopped fresh parsley

½ teaspoon finely chopped fresh dill

⅛ teaspoon grated lemon zest

Salt and black pepper

Sweet paprika

8 slices good-quality white bread, such as pain de mie

½ cup (15 g) watercress leaves

SERVES 4–6

In a heavy saucepan, combine the eggs with water to cover by 1–2 inches (2.5–5 cm) and bring to a boil over high heat. Remove from the heat, cover, and let stand for 15 minutes. Transfer the eggs to a bowl of cold water and let stand for 15 minutes to stop the cooking.

Peel the eggs and drop them into a clean bowl. Mash with a fork, then add the butter, mayonnaise, parsley, dill, and lemon zest and mix well. Season to taste with salt, pepper, and paprika.

Lay the bread slices on a work surface. Spread 4 of the slices with the egg mixture, dividing it evenly. Arrange the watercress leaves evenly over the egg mixture. Top with the remaining 4 bread slices and press firmly.

Using a serrated knife, cut off the crusts from each sandwich, then cut the sandwiches into neat fingers, triangles, or quarters.

SMOKED SALMON & DILL

½ lb (225 g) cream cheese, at room temperature

2 tablespoons finely chopped fresh dill

½ lemon

Salt and black pepper

8 slices dense whole-wheat bread

½ lb (225 g) smoked salmon, thinly sliced

SERVES 4–6

In a small bowl, combine the cream cheese and dill and mix with a fork until well blended. Season to taste with lemon juice, salt, and pepper.

Lay the bread slices on a work surface. Spread the seasoned cream cheese on the bread slices, dividing it evenly. Arrange the salmon in an even layer over 4 of the slices, then top with the remaining 4 slices, cream cheese side down.

Using a serrated knife, cut off the crusts from each sandwich, then cut each sandwich into neat fingers, triangles, or quarters.

ROAST BEEF & CHIVE

8 slices good-quality white bread, such as pain de mie

Creamy horseradish, for spreading

8 thin slices roast beef

2 tablespoons minced fresh chives

Salt and black pepper

4 leaves butter lettuce

SERVES 4−6

Lay the bread slices on a work surface. Spread each slice with a thin layer of horseradish. Top 4 of the bread slices with the roast beef slices and the chives, dividing them evenly, and season with salt and pepper. Arrange a lettuce leaf over the roast beef. Top with the remaining 4 bread slices and press firmly.

Using a serrated knife, cut off the crusts from each sandwich, then cut each sandwich into neat fingers, triangles, or quarters.

Preserves
& Spreads

QUICK STRAWBERRY JAM

Fruit preserves, particularly berry jams, are a mainstay of the afternoon tea table. Properly presented in a pretty jar or small china dish, jam in the *Downton* era would likewise have been accompanied by a designated spoon—usually small, silver, and ornately embellished with a fruit motif that signaled the flavor in the jam being served.

2 pints (700 g) strawberries, stemmed, cored, and sliced

1 cup (200 g) sugar

2 tablespoons fresh lemon juice

MAKES ABOUT 3 HALF-PINT (240-ML) JARS

Place a couple of saucers in the freezer for testing the jam.

In a heavy saucepan over medium heat, combine the strawberries, sugar, and lemon juice and bring to a boil, stirring constantly until the sugar dissolves. Reduce the heat to medium-low and cook, stirring occasionally, until the berries are tender and the juices thicken, about 10 minutes. To test if the jam is ready, remove a chilled saucer from the refrigerator, drop a small spoonful of the jam onto the saucer, and let sit for 30 seconds, then gently nudge the spoonful. If it wrinkles, the jam is ready. If it doesn't, cook for 1–2 minutes longer and test again with a clean chilled saucer.

Ladle the jam into jars and let cool. Cover and refrigerate for up to 10 days.

SYBIL: *I only need the basics. How to boil an egg, how to make tea.*

MRS. PATMORE: *Don't you know how to make tea?*

SYBIL: *Not really.*

~ SEASON 2, EPISODE 1

BLACKBERRY JAM

Some of the hedgerows around the Downton estate would likely have been loaded with blackberries from late July into September, keeping Mrs. Patmore and Daisy busy stirring pots on the stove and then packing the jam into jars for use the rest of the year. At teatime, the jam might be spread on scones or used as a filling for small tarts.

3 quarts (1.7 kg) blackberries

3 cups (600 g) sugar

¾ cup (340 ml) fresh lemon juice

MAKES 6 HALF-PINT
(240-ML) JARS

HISTORY NOTE

Estates like Downton produced much of their own food. Jams would typically be homemade, flour might be milled from the estate's own grain, and butter would come from a tenant farm.

Have ready sterilized canning jars and flat lids and screw bands (see Preserving Protocol on page 133). Place a couple of saucers in the freezer for testing the jam.

In a large nonreactive saucepan, gently toss together the berries, sugar, and lemon juice. Bring to a boil over medium-high heat, reduce the heat to medium, and cook uncovered, stirring frequently, until the jam has thickened, about 15 minutes. To test if the jam is ready, remove a chilled saucer from the refrigerator, drop a small spoonful of the jam onto the saucer, and let sit for 30 seconds, then gently nudge the spoonful. If it wrinkles, the jam is ready. If not, return the pan to the heat and boil the jam for 1–2 minutes longer, then test again with a clean chilled saucer. It will continue to thicken as it cools.

Ladle the hot jam into the jars, leaving a ¼-inch (6-mm) headspace. Slide a sterilized metal chopstick or other thin tool down the side of each jar, between the glass and jam, four or five times. This will release any air bubbles. Adjust the headspace, if necessary. Wipe the rims clean and seal tightly with the lids.

Process the jars in a boiling-water bath for 10 minutes. Transfer the jars to a folded towel and let cool completely. Check the seal on each cooled jar by pressing on the center of the lid. If the lid stays down, the seal is good. Store properly sealed jars in a cool, dark place for up to 1 year. Store any jars that failed to seal in the refrigerator for up to 3 weeks.

CURRANT JELLY

Unlike jams, which are thick and spoonable, jellies are smooth, clear spreads from which all of the fruit solids have been strained. Fresh currants are a favorite jelly ingredient, as they naturally possess the perfect amount of pectin and acidity, ensuring both a good gel without the addition of commercial pectin and a color as brilliant as the fruit.

1 lb (450 g) fresh currants

½ cup (120 ml) water

1 cup (200 g) sugar, or as needed

MAKES ONE 1 PINT (480-ML) JAR

In a large nonreactive saucepan, combine the currants and water. Bring to a boil over medium-high heat, mashing the currants with a wooden spoon or a potato masher to release their juice. Reduce the heat to low and cook uncovered, stirring frequently, until the currants are very soft, about 15 minutes.

Suspend a jelly bag over a deep nonreactive bowl and pour the currant mixture into the bag. Let the bag stand overnight or until all the juice has been expressed. Do not squeeze the bag, or the jelly will be cloudy.

The next day, place a couple of saucers in the freezer for testing the jelly. Remove the bag and discard the solids. Measure the currant juice, pour into a large nonreactive saucepan, and add an equal amount of sugar (or about 1 cup/200 g). Bring to a boil over high heat, reduce the heat to medium-high, and cook uncovered, stirring frequently and skimming off any foam that forms on the surface, until the jelly is thick enough to sheet off the back of a spoon, 10–15 minutes. Remove from the heat. To test if the jelly is ready, remove a chilled saucer from the refrigerator, drop 1 teaspoon of the jelly onto the saucer, and return it to the freezer for 2 minutes. If the mixture wrinkles when nudged gently with a finger, it is ready. If not, return the pan to the heat and boil the jelly for 1–2 minutes longer, then test again with a clean chilled saucer.

Ladle the hot jelly into a jar and let cool. Cover and refrigerate for up to 1 month.

STRAWBERRY-RHUBARB JAM

Strawberries and rhubarb are the long-awaited first sign of spring fruit. Because they are low in pectin, oranges, both the peel and the flesh, are added to give this bright-flavored, tangy jam the body it needs. Set it out with cream scones, biscuits, or crusty bread.

2 oranges, preferably blood oranges

1½–2 lb (680 g–1 kg) rhubarb, cut into ½-inch (12-mm) chunks (about 6 cups)

3 cups (420 g) strawberries, hulled and sliced

4 cups (800 g) sugar

½ cup (120 ml) fresh lemon juice

MAKES 7 HALF-PINT
(240-ML) JARS

Cut a thin slice off both ends of each orange. Cut the oranges in half crosswise and remove and discard the seeds. In a food processor, process the orange halves until roughly puréed. Transfer to a nonreactive bowl. Add the rhubarb, strawberries, and sugar to the oranges and toss gently to combine. Cover and refrigerate for at least 8 hours or up to overnight.

The next day, have ready sterilized canning jars and flat lids and screw bands (see Preserving Protocol on page 133). Place a couple of saucers in the freezer for testing the jam.

Transfer the rhubarb mixture to a large nonreactive saucepan and add the lemon juice. Bring to a boil over medium-high heat, reduce the heat to medium, and cook uncovered, stirring frequently, for 10 minutes. Remove from the heat. To test if the jam is ready, remove a chilled saucer from the refrigerator, drop a small spoonful of the jam onto the saucer, and let sit for 30 seconds, then gently nudge the spoonful. If it wrinkles, the jam is ready. If it doesn't, cook for 1–2 minutes longer and test again with a clean chilled saucer.

Ladle the hot jam into the jars, leaving a ¼-inch (6-mm) headspace. Slide a sterilized metal chopstick or other thin tool down the side of each jar, between the glass and jam, four or five times. This will release any air bubbles. Adjust the headspace, if necessary. Wipe the rims clean and seal tightly with the lids.

Process the jars in a boiling-water bath for 10 minutes. Transfer the jars to a folded towel and let cool completely. Check the seal on each cooled jar by pressing on the center of the lid. If the lid stays down, the seal is good. Store properly sealed jars in a cool, dark place for up to 1 year. Store any jars that failed to seal in the refrigerator for up to 3 weeks.

ORANGE MARMALADE

In Britain, orange marmalade has historically been prepared with bitter Seville orange, and much has been made of putting up the wildly popular preserves—a staple of both the breakfast and the teatime table—during the short Seville orange season. This recipe uses sweet oranges, but any orange variety can be used by varying the amount of sugar depending on the bitterness of the fruit.

2 lb (1 kg) oranges

8 cups (1.9 l) water

Up to 6 cups (1.2 kg) sugar

2 cups (480 ml) fresh orange juice

½ cup (120 ml) fresh lemon juice

MAKES 7 HALF-PINT (240-ML) JARS

Have ready sterilized canning jars and flat lids and screw bands (see Preserving Protocol, facing page). Place a couple of saucers in the freezer for testing the jam.

Cut a thin slice off both ends of each orange. Slice each orange crosswise as thinly as possible, preferably on a mandoline. In a large, nonreactive saucepan over medium-high heat, combine the orange slices and water and bring to a boil. Cook uncovered, stirring, for 15 minutes. Remove from the heat and let cool slightly.

Measure the orange slices and their liquid and return to the pan. For each 1 cup (240 ml), add ¾ cup (150 g) sugar to the pan. Stir in the orange and lemon juices. Bring to a boil over medium-high heat and boil rapidly for 10 minutes. Reduce the heat to medium and cook, stirring frequently, until slightly thickened and gelatinous, 7–10 minutes longer. Remove from the heat. To test if the marmalade is ready, remove a chilled saucer from the refrigerator, drop a small spoonful of the marmalade onto the saucer, and let sit for 30 seconds, then gently nudge the spoonful. If it wrinkles, the marmalade is ready. If it doesn't, cook for 1–2 minutes longer and test again with a clean chilled saucer.

Ladle the hot marmalade into the jars, leaving a ¼-inch (6-mm) headspace. Slide a metal chopstick or other thin tool down the side of each jar, between the glass and the marmalade, four or five times. This will release any air bubbles. Adjust the headspace, if necessary, then wipe the rims clean and seal tightly with the lids.

Process the jars in a boiling-water bath for 10 minutes. Transfer the jars to a folded towel and let cool completely. Check the seal on each cooled jar by pressing on the center of the lid. If the lid stays down, the seal is good. Store properly sealed jars in a cool, dark place for up to 1 year. Store any jars that failed to seal in the refrigerator for up to 3 weeks.

PRESERVING PROTOCOL

To sterilize jars for holding preserves, first wash the jars with hot, soapy water.
Put the clean jars upright in a large pot, add hot water to cover by 2 inches
(5 cm), and bring to a boil over high heat. Boil the water for 15 minutes,
then turn off the heat. The jars can remain in the hot water for up to 1 hour.
Using a jar lifter or tongs, lift out the jars, draining them well, and set aside
on a kitchen towel to dry. To sterilize two-part canning lids—rubber-lined lid
and screw band—sterilize them in simmering (not boiling) water for 10 minutes.

If a recipe calls for a boiling-water bath, use the same pot and water you used for
sterilizing the jars. Put a rack on the bottom of the pot and bring the water to a boil.
Using a jar lifter or tongs, lower the filled jars onto the rack, spacing them about
½ inch (12 mm) apart. The water should cover the jars by 2 inches (5 cm);
add more boiling water if needed. Bring to a rolling boil, cover, and boil for
10 minutes. Turn off the heat and let the jars sit for about 10 minutes before
removing them from the pot and setting them aside to dry.

LEMON CURD

The term *lemon curd* has a long history in British culinary tradition, though its meaning has varied over the years. Early on, it meant literally curds—or cheese—arrived at by adding lemon juice to fresh cream and then separating the curds from the whey. What remains a mystery is when those simple curds became the creamy citrus custard made from lemon juice, eggs, and butter that was served at Downton—and is still served today.

1 whole egg

4 egg yolks

½ cup (100 g) sugar

⅓ cup (80 ml) fresh lemon juice

2 tablespoons unsalted butter, cubed

MAKES ABOUT 1 CUP (250 G)

In a heatproof bowl set over (not touching) barely simmering water in a saucepan, whisk together the whole egg, egg yolks, sugar, and lemon juice. Cook, stirring constantly, until thickened, 5–8 minutes. To test if it is ready, pull the spoon out of the bowl and draw your finger across the back of it; if your finger leaves a trail that does not fill in immediately, the curd is ready.

Remove from the heat and add the butter, stirring until incorporated. Strain through a fine-mesh sieve into another bowl. Cover with plastic wrap, pressing the plastic directly onto the surface of the curd (this helps prevent a skin from forming). Refrigerate until well chilled and set, about 3 hours, before using. The curd will keep in an airtight container in the refrigerator for up to 1 week.

MOCK CLOTTED CREAM

Clotted cream is a requisite component of a proper English cream tea and a classic accompaniment to scones. Prized for its natural thick consistency and mild nutty flavor, it is produced in Devon and Cornwall, where it is known as Devonshire cream and Cornish cream respectively. It is made by heating unpasteurized milk until a thick layer of cream forms on its surface and then skimming off the cream layer once the milk has cooled. Although no combination of ingredients can replicate the unique flavor and consistency of true clotted cream, this mock recipe, which mixes mascarpone cheese with heavy cream, is a respectable substitute.

½ cup (120 ml) heavy cream

1 cup (225 g) mascarpone cheese, at room temperature

1 tablespoon confectioners' sugar, or to taste

MAKES ABOUT 1 CUP (250 G)

In a bowl, using an electric mixer, beat the cream on medium-high speed until soft peaks form. On medium speed, add the mascarpone and sugar and beat until incorporated. Taste, then adjust with more sugar if needed. Serve at once.

TEA ETIQUETTE

Both Cornwall and Devon lay claim to the invention of the cream tea, which consists of scones with clotted cream and fruit jams (preserves) served along with the tea. The residents of each county have strong views on the order of the preserves and cream. The Devonshire tradition is cream first with preserves spread on top, while the Cornish tradition is preserves first with the cream on top. For everyone else, the order remains one of personal preference.

INDEX

VIOLET:

Then there's nothing more to be said.
Are we going to have tea? Or not?

~ SEASON 1, EPISODE 3

weldon**owen**

Publisher **Roger Shaw**
Associate Publisher **Amy Marr**
Creative Director **Chrissy Kwasnik**
Art Director **Bronwyn Lane**
Photography Director & Designer **Lisa Berman**
Managing Editor **Tarji Rodriguez**
Production Manager **Binh Au**

Food Photographer **John Kernick**
Food Stylist **Cyd Raftus McDowell**
Prop Stylist **Suzie Myers**
Cover Illustration **Conor Buckley**

Produced by Weldon Owen International
1150 Brickyard Cove Road
Richmond, CA 94801
www.weldonowen.com

Printed and bound in China

First printed in 2020
10 9 8 7 6 5 4 3

Library of Congress Cataloging-in-Publication
data is available.

ISBN: 978-1-68188-503-2

INTRODUCTORY TEXT BY **REGULA YSEWIJN**

**WELDON OWEN WISHES TO THANK
THE FOLLOWING PEOPLE FOR THEIR
GENEROUS SUPPORT IN PRODUCING THIS BOOK**

Julian Fellowes, Rizwan Alvi, Lisa Atwood, Antoinette Cardoza, Manuel Cardoza,
Abigail Dodge, Mimi Freund, Annie Gray, Charlotte Havelange, Rachel Markowitz,
Elizabeth Parson, Nico Sherman, Sharon Silva, and Josh Simons

CARNIVAL FILMS
Gareth Neame, Aliboo Bradbury, Charlotte Fay, and Nion Hazell

PETERS FRASER AND DUNLOP
Annabel Merullo and Laura McNeill